Using Curriculum Mapping & Assessment Data to Improve Learning

Bena Kallick ▪ **Jeff Colosimo**
Foreword by Heidi Hayes Jacobs

CORWIN
PRESS
A SAGE Company

For information:

Corwin Press
A SAGE Company
2455 Teller Road
Thousand Oaks, California 91320
www.corwinpress.com

SAGE Ltd.
1 Oliver's Yard
55 City Road
London, EC1Y 1SP
United Kingdom

SAGE India Pvt. Ltd.
B 1/I 1 Mohan Cooperative
Industrial Area
Mathura Road, New Delhi 110 044
India

SAGE Asia-Pacific Pte. Ltd.
33 Pekin Street #02-01
Far East Square
Singapore 048763

Printed in the United States of America

Library of Congress Cataloging-in-Publication Data

Kallick, Bena.
  Using curriculum mapping and assessment data to improve learning /
Bena Kallick, Jeff Colosimo.
      p. cm.
  Includes bibliographical references and index.
  ISBN 978-1-4129-2781-9 (cloth) — ISBN 978-1-4129-2782-6 (pbk.)
1. Curriculum planning. 2. Curriculum evaluation. 3. Teacher participation in
curriculum planning. 4. School improvement programs.
I. Colosimo, Jeff. II. Title.

  LB2806.15.K35 2009
  375'.001—dc22

2008004903

This book is printed on acid-free paper.

08 09 10 11 10 9 8 7 6 5 4 3 2 1

Acquisitions Editor: Cathy Hernandez
Editorial Assistants: Megan Bedell and Ena Rosen
Production Editor: Appingo Publishing Services
Cover Designer: Lisa Miller

Contents

Foreword

Navigation strategies are requisite for a voyage that brings curriculum mapping and assessment analysis together on the same ship. Not only does data from multiple sources provide educators with a compass for bringing all members of your school community together to plan effective directions for your voyage and for your learners, but it is does so realistically. This book is a remarkable and necessary contribution to the mapping work that now reaches all over the globe.

Kallick and Colosimo have collaborated to bring the reader detailed coaching on sophisticated "how to's" in the mapping review process. You will find assistance on helping faculty engage as a team and a system in establishing key purposes for mapping; you will come to the "intersection of curriculum and assessment" and know how to merge your faculties' findings in both areas to close the achievement gap; you will learn how to employ the reports that emerge from curriculum mapping software to create meaningful consensus; you will learn how to create a culture of possibility and engagement.

The three case studies presented do more than reinforce the contentions raised in the book; they shed light on critical junctures. Tribuzzi, Wiley, Graham, and Cleveland recommend patience and determination and ground the idea of long-term adjustment but steady growth in their experience with a suburban district in upstate New York. Of particular note is "the data pipeline" advocated by Boegly in her chapter on the gains made at her elementary school, which elevates and elaborates on the critical role of the principal in leading for change. Dunlap's work in West Chester, Pennsylvania, has received national attention as he enthusiastically not only develops a far reaching professional development plan for his high school, but also suggests how his faculty now has taken the lead in integrating literacy into every classroom as part of the mapping process.

Bena Kallick has a reputation nationally and internationally as one of the most subtle and nuanced thinkers and practitioners of reflective systems work. She knows how to help people "bring it all together" with her extensive research and her profound sense of what matters most for learners and their teachers. Jeff Colosimo is respected for his grounded and spirited sense of how to help educators, business people, and political leadership join together to create the best kind of support tools to help schools achieve their goals. They are a terrific team and they have created a terrific book to help you consider your next steps and your larger visions using curriculum mapping, assessment, and technology to generate vibrant and productive learning communities in your education setting.

—Heidi Hayes Jacobs, EdD

Preface

Three questions are at the center of our work toward improving student achievement:

1. What do we want students to know and be able to do?
2. What evidence do we have that they are learning what we have identified?
3. What do we do with what we learn about their learning to help them grow and improve? (DuFour, Eaker, & DuFour, 2005)

Traditionally, we have used parallel assessment, curriculum development, and management processes to answer these questions. We have studied our student learning by examining the results of state, national, and local assessments. In addition, school committees have worked on the development and revision of curriculum, which has often resulted in the purchase of new textbooks or programs. However, in many of our systems, these processes have been separate and disconnected rather than intersected and building on one another.

All of the information that can be extracted from our assessment and curriculum processes could be defined as data. With advances in technology, the ability to access this type of data has been completely transformed. Our tired minds must no longer confront and try to make sense of dozens of papers and reports coded with numbers. Now with Web-based access to bar charts, pie charts, and other means of transforming the raw numbers into meaningful data, we can more easily identify patterns and trends. With those summaries in front of us, the time we might have spent counting and sorting can instead be used for professional dialogue about the meaning of the data. This focus on using data as the basis for making decisions will help us answer the third question—what do we need to do to improve student learning—and needs to exist at every level of the organization.

- Classroom teachers need to be able to make decisions that affect their daily instruction.
- Grade, course, and department groups need to make decisions that collectively will affect the way their courses of study are designed.
- Building-level teachers and administrators need to have a dialogue about the important narrative of a student's journey longitudinally across time.

- Conversations about building-level decisions need to occur across buildings.
- And finally, central administration needs to communicate the wisdom that has been gleaned from all of the conversations, and make systemic decisions about change.

What has propelled the emphasis on accountability are explicit statements of performance against standards from both state and national organizations, including state departments of education. Standards that were perhaps previously tacit and may or may not have been operating in individual classrooms now have become explicitly stated and agreed upon across an entire district. However, the transition to standards-based schools has not been without struggle. Attempting to provide clarity of expectations, as well as determining how student performance should be measured, has led to frequent changes of direction in curriculum and instructional methods. We currently have named more standards than can ever be addressed in 12 years of schooling (Marzano & Kendall, 1998).

The hard work of becoming effective, standards-based schools continues. Feedback from educators has led many states to develop performance indicators that break down the larger, conceptual standards statements they originally endorsed. This work is deeply associated with our value systems since the standards are statements of what we most value for students to learn. The process of breaking down the standards and naming developmental stages for performance has led educators to wrestle with when and how these standards are best attained and how they are best measured.

As this dilemma between districts and states continues, children keep pouring into our schools. We cannot wait for differences to be settled. Hence, schools take an active position with this work. Many schools engage in the process of identifying what they consider to be "power standards"—those standards that are most enduring, provide leverage for next year's work, and provide the best opportunities for interdisciplinary connections (Ainsworth, 2003). This process helps to narrow what is required in a standards-based curriculum. Another significant practice has been for teachers to come together to work on aligning their curriculum to standards.

At the same time that standards were becoming the currency of conversations about curriculum, Heidi Hayes Jacobs provided a model for analyzing curriculum—curriculum mapping (Jacobs, 1997). Her work introduced a method for seeing curriculum as data. Rather than using the traditional curriculum guides that are so text heavy that they would be difficult to analyze, Jacobs' model shows educators how to break the curriculum into categories such as essential questions, content, skills, and assessments. This process of developing curriculum maps provides a new and effective method for examining the taught curriculum. By creating a curriculum map that is separated into data, we are able to unpack a given standard for the purpose of alignment. Once again, advances in technology have accelerated this process so that each element of the curriculum can now be separated into individually accessible and searchable data fields.

Figure 0.1 Example of a Curriculum Map

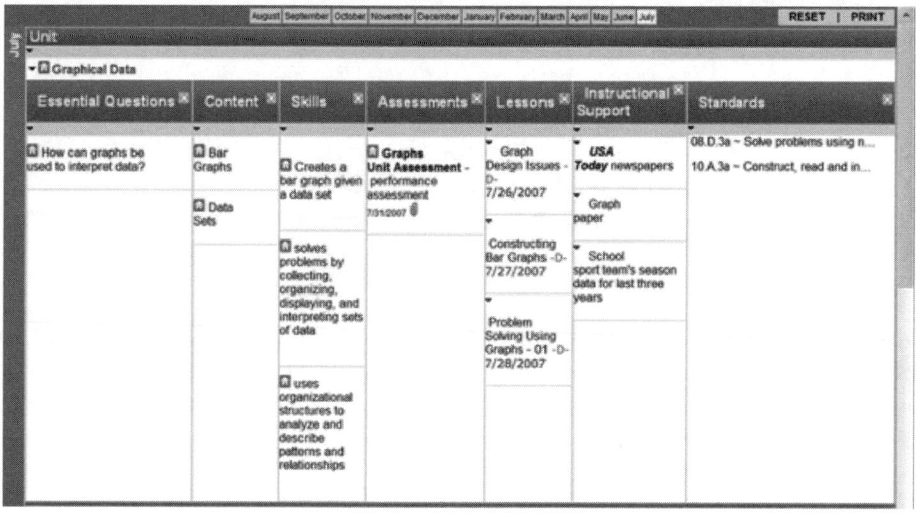

© Performance Pathways. Used with permission.

Curriculum is analyzed to find gaps—are there standards that have not been addressed? Repetitions—are there topics in content that repeat without any significant changes in the material? Spirals—places where the curriculum spirals and builds in complexity? Are thinking skills focused and to what level? These curriculum conversations help us to answer the first question—what is it that we want students to know and be able to do?

The second question, what evidence do we have that tells us about how well students are measuring up to standards, is answered by an analysis of assessment results. Once again, with technology as a tool, we are able to easily access charts and graphs that aggregate and disaggregate data from national, state, district, and classroom assessments. We are able to see a more complete picture of student performance by looking at a student's portfolio of assessment results across time.

This book provides some possible intersecting paths for answering the three fundamental questions. We show examples of how maps are used to examine and revise curriculum; how assessment data is organized and displayed so that the data can be examined to determine what

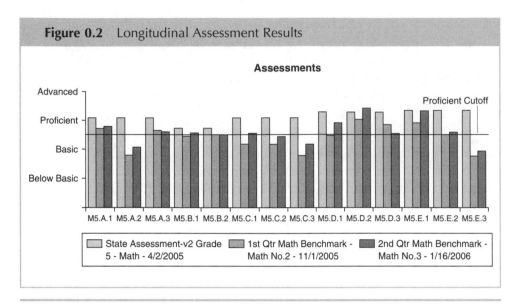

Figure 0.2 Longitudinal Assessment Results

© Performance Pathways. Used with permission.

changes in curriculum and instruction need to take place; suggestions about professional dialogue show how schools are attempting to answer the third question. The end result is to show the intersection between curriculum and assessment data that is necessary to make data-informed decisions.

The first chapter provides an introduction to a vision for this work, and the required elements of change within an organization to support this vision. It addresses the important questions that are always asked: Why are we doing this? What is the purpose of this work? What can we expect the outcomes might be? Is this a plan of the day or will it be sustained over time?

The second chapter focuses on the critical role the proper incentives play in changing the culture so that the work can be sustained. We look at some practices that contributed to successful implementation of new practices. In this chapter we also explore how the data serves as an important vehicle for establishing leadership in the schools with particular attention to distributing leadership throughout the system.

In the third chapter we explore the data sources for curriculum and assessment and then show ways to maximize the intersection of those sources for more informed decision-making. The possibilities for analysis of data lead to the fourth chapter in which we provide protocols to help facilitate the conversations among educators regarding the data. Although the results can be provided with numbers, patterns, and trends, ultimately the conversations that focus on a close examination of this information is at the heart of the potential to change curriculum, instruction, and assessment to the benefit of student achievement.

Chapters 5 through 7 offer case studies. The stories from the field are honest and rich. They offer an opportunity for learning as the authors describe their visions, how they brought their work successfully to their districts, and how they sustained their work over time.

Finally, we address the challenges that we continue to face and some tips on how to meet those challenges in Chapter 8. This is hard work—we appreciate the many people who have joined us in the work to make this book possible.

Acknowledgments

Corwin Press gratefully acknowledges the contributions of the following reviewers:

Kenneth M. Arndt
Superintendent
Community Unit School District 300
Carpentersville, IL

Victoria L. Bernhardt
Executive Director
Education for the Future
Chico, CA

Marie Blum
Superintendent
Canaseraga Central School District
Canaseraga, NY

Edie Holcomb
Former Teacher, Principal, District Administrator
Education Consultant and Author
Bellingham, WA

Ronald L. Russell
Associate Director
Loess Hills Area Education Agency 13
Shenandoah, IA (Southwest Iowa Region)

David A. Squires
Associate Professor
Southern Connecticut State University
New Haven, CT

Susan Udelhofen
Education Consultant
SU-Consulting
Madison, WI

About the Authors

Bena Kallick, PhD, is a private consultant providing services to school districts, state departments of education, professional organizations, and public agencies throughout the United States and abroad. Kallick received her doctorate in educational evaluation at Union Graduate School. Her areas of focus include group dynamics, creative and critical thinking, and alternative assessment strategies for the classroom. Her written work includes *Literature to Think About* (a whole language curriculum); *Changing Schools into Communities for Thinking; Assessment in the Learning Organization and Habits of Mind* (a four-book series), coauthored with Arthur Costa; *Strategies for Self-Directed Learning* (published by Corwin Press); and *Information Technology for Schools*, coauthored with James Wilson.

Formerly a Teachers' Center director, Kallick also created a children's museum based on problem solving and invention. She was the coordinator of a high school alternative designed for at-risk students. She is cofounder of Performance Pathways, a company dedicated to providing easy-to-use software for curriculum mapping and assessment tracking and reporting, an integrated suite. Kallick's teaching appointments have included Yale University School of Organization and Management, University of Massachusetts Center for Creative and Critical Thinking, and Union Graduate School. She was formerly on the Board of the Apple Foundation, the Board of Jobs for the Future, and is presently on the Board for Learning Effects and Weston Woods Institute.

Jeff Colosimo is a cofounder and the current CEO of Performance Pathways Inc., a technology company specializing in data-driven curriculum and assessment solutions. Colosimo has become a nationally recognized business leader and successful entrepreneur as a result of his commitment and innovative work over the past 15 years in the K–12 education technologies industry. In his past experience as the founder and president of two other technology companies, AlterNet Performance and Alternate Solutions, his innovative work in the field led to several awards, including Ernst and Young's Entrepreneur of the Year in 1997, Arthur Anderson's Best Practices Award in 1998, and a "Top 100 Hot Emerging Company" national ranking by *Computer World* magazine in 1998.

Currently as the president of Performance Pathways, he leads a team of technology professionals that develop and implement data-driven technologies for school districts. Their products help districts utilize curriculum and assessment data to increase student achievement.

1

Transforming to a Data-Informed Culture

The future is not a result of choices among alternative paths offered by the present, but a place that is created—created first in mind and will, created next in activity. The future is not some place we are going to, but one we are creating. The paths are not to be found, but made, and the activity of making them changes both the maker and the destination.

—John Schaar

If you don't have a clear sense of where you are going, it is easy to lose your way. If the vision within an organization cannot be translated into practical terms, it will also lose its way. Given there is a desire to change the way we use data to increase student achievement, Ambrose suggests there are key ingredients that lead to systemic change—a set of elements that guide the path for change (Ambrose, 1996). The elements include a shared **vision** in the organization and people in the organization who are **skillful** enough to realize what the vision implies in practical terms. It is necessary that there be an **incentive** for doing the work, the required **resources** available, and an **action plan** that provides confidence the work will proceed and not just be another false start.

In this chapter we will consider the need for a shared vision and then examine the resources required to realize the vision. We follow with an action plan that includes building the skills of the educators as well as attending to necessary resources. We also place special attention on the role of technology, as it is a critical resource for accomplishing this work.

CREATING A VISION

Imagining what is possible and aiming for the most positive vision of what should be done to create a data-informed culture is a necessary first step. The vision provides clarity about where the district is going and why it is purposefully moving in that direction. In our work, we use Figure 1.1 to represent a vision of the intersection of assessment and curriculum data that will lead to making better decisions about how to increase student achievement.

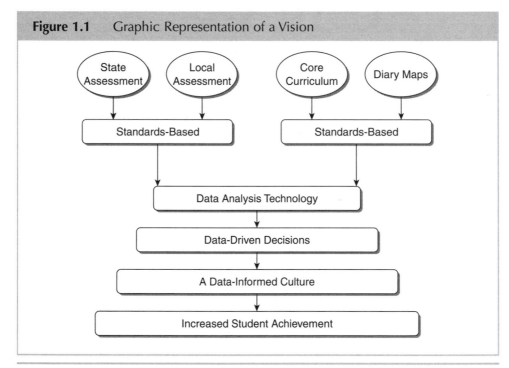

Figure 1.1 Graphic Representation of a Vision

© Performance Pathways. Used with permission.

In Figure 1.1, the vision is divided into five clear statements:

- We may start with a foundation of standards-based assessment and curriculum data from multiple perspectives.
- We must use technology as a tool to help us.
- Data will drive our decisions.
- Informed decisions (based on that data) will ultimately be made about assessment and curriculum.
- The end goal is increased student achievement.

Our graphic suggests that improvements in student achievement can never be attributed to any one single factor or any one program. Instead, there are clusters of factors that build upon one another to contribute to sustained improvement. It is not assessment and curriculum in isolation, but a combination of people, technology, and processes that will ultimately achieve the goal. The vision is a diagram of process that shows the movement from assessment and curriculum data that are standards-based on to the intersection of the data in which assessment and curriculum are analyzed and ultimately provide the basis for informed decisions that will increase student performance.

Our experience tells us that making this vision operational requires

- specific, observable, and measurable proficiencies;
- a sustained collection of performance data and analysis of those data horizontally, vertically, and longitudinally among the people responsible for instruction;
- adjustments to curriculum, instruction, and assessment based on the analysis;
- planning time on a regular basis for review of student performance among the people who share the care and instruction for the target population;
- sufficient time to allow for sustained growth among the students.

This list should be taken into consideration when administrators develop a school improvement plan. In addition to a clear vision, the plan must be certain to address the **professional development** needs teachers might have to develop skills for the analysis of data; the **technology** resources required to provide a good summary of information from the data entered; a **clear understanding** among the professional staff about why and how this work will benefit themselves and ultimately students; and a monitoring system tied to an **action plan** so that modifications can take place in a timely fashion. If a district puts all these key factors in place for school improvement, it is poised for creating the necessary changes needed to improve student performance.

CURRICULUM MAPPING AS A DATA SOURCE

Over the past 15 years there has been a shift in the typical approach for developing and maintaining curriculum. Schools have always had curriculum guides, which we will refer to as the **written curriculum**. The assumption has been that the guides are followed. However, many teachers, by necessity or by choice, redesigned the curriculum to fit their own classroom and the needs of their students. Curriculum committees made decisions based on representatives from various grade levels and courses. Those decisions were usually more impressionistic than data driven. We typically did not report to each other about what was changed and why those decisions were made. As a result, teachers were often unaware of what was taking place in another teacher's building or classroom.

As schools began to audit their curriculum for accreditation, they realized there was often a difference between the **written curriculum** and the **taught curriculum.** Teachers made decisions individually about what was to be taught and when it was to be taught. Heidi Hayes Jacobs addressed this issue and provided a process—curriculum mapping—for developing a dynamic curriculum, one that takes into account the discrepancies that might occur between the written and the taught curriculum (Jacobs, 1997).

Jacobs has defined critical aspects of mapping and provided a key set of principles. Her model suggests that curriculum is mapped according to the calendar year and reflects the operational or taught curriculum. This ensures the curriculum is revised based on authentic data. Assessment data offer a lens for examining the learned curriculum. The mapping process requires that teachers address the continuity of curriculum from grade to grade, building to building, year to year. Each teacher maps his or her own classroom curriculum, and then engages in the process of comparing those maps to the maps of other teachers. Through this type of review, we develop a clear picture of what our students are exposed to. The process of comparing what the written curriculum states with what the operational curriculum reflects usually leads to the discovery of many gaps and repetitions, and has resulted in powerful conversations among teachers about the pedagogical values that are underpinning curricular decisions.

Key to all mapping is the dynamic way that curriculum will continuously be reviewed, revised, and renewed. However, as mapping practices have evolved, districts determined their own entry points for mapping. Many schools started by having teachers individually map their operational curriculum. Then, through an extensive "Read Through" process, teachers came to consensus about what was essential for a course of study. They developed maps named Consensus, Essential, or CORE that became the points of agreement for teachers in the district. All teachers teach what has been deemed CORE; however, flexibility within CORE is determined by the way the teacher responds to the students in her classroom. The flexibility of curriculum is usually expressed through lessons, assessments, enhancements, and modifications.

Most districts have already been revising their curriculum based on standards. As a result, when embarking upon a curriculum mapping initiative, many believed they had already started to build a CORE curriculum. These schools began mapping by first recording the CORE curriculum, as determined by a representative team of educators. The recorded CORE curriculum is then enhanced through teacher-centered diary mapping efforts. Figure 1.2 shows a range of possible ways districts have determined what is CORE.

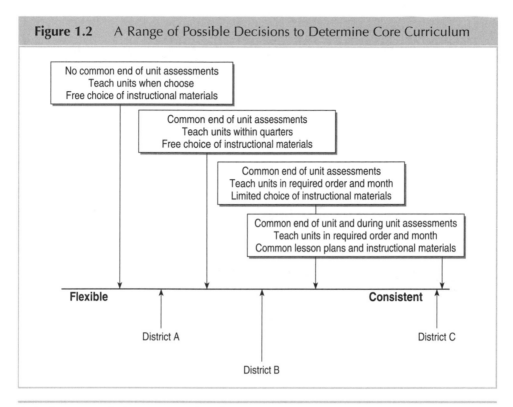

Figure 1.2   A Range of Possible Decisions to Determine Core Curriculum

No common end of unit assessments
Teach units when choose
Free choice of instructional materials

Common end of unit assessments
Teach units within quarters
Free choice of instructional materials

Common end of unit assessments
Teach units in required order and month
Limited choice of instructional materials

Common end of unit and during unit assessments
Teach units in required order and month
Common lesson plans and instructional materials

Flexible   Consistent

District A   District C

District B

ASSESSMENT RESULTS AS A DATA SOURCE

Curriculum mapping, regardless of approach, provides a forum for exchanging information about practices based on real classroom data. This data, when taken into account with assessment data, can be the basis for informed decisions to improve student learning. Traditionally, assessments have been an afterthought to curriculum. In many instances, assessment was considered separate from curriculum. Schools had a director of assessment who might not even meet with curriculum directors. Teachers would instruct and then announce a test to their students. Assessments were considered the caboose of the train rather than the engine that fueled curriculum and instruction.

Educators quickly learned that initiatives to improve student achievement cannot be based on a once per year test. In addition, as we place a greater emphasis on using data, educators begin to realize that there is very little comparable data to examine beyond standardized or state tests. Classroom teachers usually design their own assessments, so the results from class to class in a given course might vary. Although everyone may claim they are teaching to the standards, measures of performance are not often tied to the standards with any specificity. This issue has led to the development of benchmark assessments, tied to standards that are given to all students in the course or grade level. These assessments provide a district with more information than their state assessment. For example, as assessment items are individually aligned to standards and the information is readily available, item-analysis reports and efforts can yield a more in-depth perspective of student performance. At this point, most schools understand the significance of monitoring valid, standards-based local assessments to develop predictive strategies, and to help determine changes in curriculum and classroom instruction.

USING AN ACTION PLAN TO MONITOR PROCESS

One of the biggest challenges in education is ensuring that our key initiatives do not lose their way due to changes in administration or just poor planning practices. Given the busy schedules of most schools, an action plan can serve as a discipline for staying on track. It also serves as a clear statement of who is responsible for what, so that progress can be celebrated and the momentum for improvement is sustained. At a minimum, the following elements are key to the development of an action plan:

1. An action plan should be a tangible document monitored throughout the planning process. It should be a living document that can be used to manage and monitor progress toward an established, well understood, and measurable goal. An action plan that is not documented and accessible in an electronic format or at least on paper can easily be lost in highly individual interpretations and memories. As a result, the loss of what actually took place can easily lead to a false start.

2. Keep your plans brief and to the point, so the process of updating the plan via project status meetings does not become overwhelming. We often spend too much time focusing on the written content of the plan instead of the definitive actions required for success of the plan. The main purpose of an action plan is for task management and status monitoring, not facilitating discussions or debate.

3. All actions plans must tie to the vision. The plan may become tiered with specific tasks identified at multiple levels within a district, but the vision should be the glue that keeps everything

connected. For example, a district action plan for student achievement is not just the superintendent's plan; it is the plan for all building administrators, classes, and ultimately teachers. If all action plans are tied to the vision and constructed in this manner, we have a much better chance of creating systemic change as needed. If this type of understanding exists, the foundation for an effective planning process is set.

4. Begin and end the action plan with the same goal statement. The goal must be established and agreed upon in a collaborative manner, as it is easier to support an initiative when it is cultivated from the bottom up. Although it may be initially easier for an administrator to independently create the goal statement, the initiative will be in jeopardy from the beginning because it is subject to the position or status of that administrator at that given moment. Unfortunately most goals are created by district superintendents or building principals in isolation in an effort to quickly make an impact, or just because of the amount of effort required within the culture of a district to gain consensus on the goal.

5. When writing a goal statement it must be structured and presented in a clear and concise manner. Consider using a "SMART" approach when creating goal statements. SMART is an acronym for the following:

S – Specific
M – Measurable
A – Attainable
R – Realistic
T – Time-driven

For example, a district whose goal statement reads, "we will increase student achievement," did not develop a SMART goal. With a little work, the goal can be revised into the following SMART format: "Our goal is to increase our fifth grade math state assessment results from 45% to 54% proficiency."

This goal is (S)specific to a grade and subject, (M)measurable based on proficiency levels, (A)attainable with the consensus of building staff, (R)realistic based on statistics from other comparable districts, and (T)time-driven as everyone is aware of the date for the next assessment. A SMART goal in this format can easily be supported by an action plan and an effective planning process.

Once an appropriate goal statement is developed, an action plan is more easily built, understood, and followed. Although there is no incorrect format for an action plan, it should contain, at a minimum, the following components:

- a series of tasks tied to the goal that, if met, will lead to success;
- assigned and dedicated individuals who will be responsible for each task; and
- target dates for the completion of each task.

An effective action planning process can help an organization change and become a data-informed culture that uses both assessment and curriculum data to revise instruction and increase student achievement. Two examples of action plans are shown in Figure 1.3 and Table 1.1. One is from the New Hampshire Department of Education, and the other is from the Boyertown Area School District, located in Pennsylvania. The first is a plan to implement a statewide data-analysis tool for assessment data. The second is a rollout of technology for accessing reports based on assessment data. The two plans are obviously different in size and scope, and, at first glance, appear to look completely different. However, both plans contain the necessary core elements of an effective plan and, as a result, led to successful implementations of their solution.

Figure 1.3 Project Plan for State of New Hampshire

Task Name	Duration	Start	Finish	Resource Names
⊟ **Phase One Project Implementation**	**99.4 days?**	**Tue 10/10/06**	**Tue 2/27/07**	
Initiation Phase	0 days	Wed 10/11/06	Wed 10/11/06	
⊟ Project Preparation	1.3 days	Wed 10/11/06	Thu 10/12/06	
Assign PPI Project Team - IP	13 hrs	Wed 10/11/06	Thu 10/12/06	PPI Mgmt,Project Manager
Verify Client Project Team - IP	0 hrs	Wed 10/11/06	Wed 10/11/06	Project Manager,PPI Mgmt
Schedule Implementation Meeting - IP	8 hrs	Wed 10/11/06 ▼	Wed 10/11/06	Cust Serv Org
⊟ Implementation Meeting	2 days	Tue 10/10/06	Thu 10/12/06	
Review Project Scope and Vision - IP	10 hrs	Tue 10/10/06	Thu 10/12/06	Project Manager
Team Introductions - IP	0 hrs	Wed 10/11/06	Wed 10/11/06	Project Manager
Review Project Tasks - IP	0 hrs	Wed 10/11/06	Wed 10/11/06	Project Manager
Review Project Timeline- IP	0 hrs	Wed 10/11/06	Wed 10/11/06	Project Manager
Assign Resources - IP	0 hrs	Wed 10/11/06	Wed 10/11/06	Project Manager
Project Manager Staff Preparation Meeting - IP	1 day	Fri 10/13/06	Fri 10/13/06	Project Manager
Assessment Staff Preparation Meeting - IP	1 day	Mon 10/16/06	Mon 10/16/06	Ed Consultant
Data Staff Preparation Meeting - IP	1 day	Tue 10/17/06	Tue 10/17/06	Data Specialist
Technology Staff Preparation Meeting - IP	1 day	Fri 10/13/06	Fri 10/13/06	SW Dev Consultant
Training Staff Preparation Meeting - IP	1 day	Thu 10/19/06	Thu 10/19/06	Trainer
Status Meeting - Init Phase - IP	1 day	Mon 10/23/06	Mon 10/23/06	Project Manager,Ed Consultant

Credit: Mary Heath

Table 1.1   Boyertown Area School District—Data Analysis Technology Rollout, 2006–2007

Date	Time	Content/Action Step	Person(s) Responsible
December 21, 2006	3:00– 5:00	Extended overview of product to core group of administrators and teachers.	Stephanie Gladfelter Robert Scoboria Susan Keck Special Ed Directors
January 15, 2007	8:00– 12:00	½ day training for all administrators and Marca Malick (POC). Data teams need to be identified by March 28. Training will be week of August 13.	Dara Bogovic Marty Horner Susan Keck
January 24, 2007	9:00– 10:00	Follow up activities for administrators during Leadership Team Meeting.	Susan Keck
February 16, 2007	7:30– 8:30	Overview of IEP product to all Special Education Teachers.	Stephanie Gladfelter Robert Scoboria Susan Keck Special Ed Directors
February 16, 2007	8:45– 11:45	Follow up ½ day training for all administrators and Marca Malick (POC).	Dara Bogovic Marty Horner Susan Keck
February 28, 2007	9:00– 10:00	Facilitating conversations around data. Leadership Team Meeting. Principals identify data teams from each building. Approx imately 6–12 per team.	Susan Keck Principals
March 28, 2007		Principals forward names of data teams to Susan Keck.	Principals Susan Keck
April 4, 2007	12:30– 1:30	Overview of solution and the role of data for entire BASD staff. Two separate but simultaneous presentations (elementary and secondary groups).	Dara Bogovic Marty Horner Susan Keck

Credit: Susan Keck

TECHNOLOGY AS A RESOURCE

As demands increase for all educators, so does the need for additional tools and resources. This new cyclical approach of creating and revising curriculum, instruction, and assessment requires the use of technology. Schools cannot maintain the necessary dynamic relationships without the aid of technology.

Technology can provide easy access to curriculum and assessment data for all educators from classroom teachers to district administrators. By making data widely available, technology can facilitate collaboration about curriculum and assessment. Using technology to store, access, and review data helps ensure that data becomes the basis for our dialogue. This will lead to deeper and more informed professional conversations, and can have a profound effect on the educational environment.

We suggested earlier that in order to sustain organizational change it is essential to provide the necessary resources for people to do the work. Technology is a necessary resource. As Collins suggests in *Good to Great* (Collins, 2001), technology is an accelerator of momentum. Once a user reaches a proficient level of using technology, data is easily accessed and time can now be applied to more appropriate efforts. Instead of spending time counting and sorting, the professional community spends time analyzing and making sense out of the information. While the work can still be rigorous and time consuming, when curriculum and instruction change to the benefit of student learning, the momentum to do the work will increase. When it reaches the point of being used systemically by all educators in the organization, technology will become a key resource that transforms the district into a data-informed culture.

SUMMARY

Our approach to data-informed decision-making is to develop a series of changes that lead to building a sustained foundation for a data-informed culture. A vision is created and lived throughout the district. The vision emphasizes the use of curriculum and assessment data in an environment where data dialogue occurs on a regular basis. Goals are established, monitored, and reviewed on a regular basis. And data dialogue occurs in all aspects of the educational system. The key components include knowledge about curriculum and assessment data, utilizing technology to provide summarized information from the data, using the data as the basis for inquiry about student learning, and developing an action plan to test the hypotheses that have been generated. The most difficult part of this work is to sustain the culture as administrators, Boards of Education, and teachers change. Our experience suggests that a carefully monitored and revised action plan can serve as a reminder and discipline for continuing the work regardless of the leadership.

2 Transforming the Culture Through Incentives

According to one definition, culture "is a shared, learned, symbolic system of values, beliefs, and attitudes that shapes and influences perception and behavior"—an abstract "mental blueprint" or "mental code" (Dahl, 2007). As we consider the issues at stake in transforming a culture, we must look at where the possible leverage is that will have transformative value. One of the key elements that we identified in Chapter 1 is that the vision of the organization must be shared. We are suggesting that the existing culture of the organization must have a shared vision about collecting, analyzing, and using data to inform decisions. Since culture is a shared and learned system of values, beliefs, and attitudes, representation of those values, beliefs, and attitudes must be present in all actions of the organization. We have discussed how a graphic representation of the vision can serve as a symbolic reminder of the organizational culture. In addition, we explore how an action plan based on the vision will make the vision operational and will cultivate new behaviors in the culture. In this chapter, we suggest two additional key leverage points that serve as incentives for changes in behavior: the way we use time and the way we formalize new roles.

TIME AS AN INCENTIVE

Most teachers are clear about the use of time in schools—there is simply not enough time to do what they are expected to do! When adding the significance of using data to improve student achievement, one of the best incentives for doing this work is to provide additional time to analyze the data. This activity cannot just be assigned. You must provide real time for taking on this challenge. Many districts are making certain that there is time for professional learning communities to meet. This usually takes place once or twice a month. The focus is on the three fundamental questions that we referred to in the introduction:

- What do you want students to know and be able to do?
- What evidence do you have that they are achieving?
- What are you doing about students who are not achieving?

It is clear that these communities keep the focus on curriculum, instruction, and assessment. It is also clear that the data from curriculum maps and assessment performances is essential to the conversation.

We have also found that there is a value to organizing time for these purposes:

- Short, regular meetings within a grade level or course so that teachers can consistently engage with data and instructional decision making
- Meetings within the building that focus on across-grade or department discussions that are a bit longer and allow teachers time to consider curriculum and assessment data longitudinally. For example, given the assessment results being studied, what were the prerequisite skills that were necessary for success? Where do those skills appear in the maps? Is there a continuity of teaching and reinforcing across the years that provides a solid scaffold for student performance?
- All day professional development experiences where teachers have the opportunity to work across buildings throughout the system. These meetings focus on a system picture—where are there differences in buildings and how does the group understand that? For example, when three elementary buildings feed to the same middle school, what is the effect on the middle school when there is no consistency among the elementary buildings? The focus is on assessment data and how that data helps the group analyze differences in the focus of the curriculum. Often a department will meet K–12 so that they can talk about the consistency of curriculum based on assessment data. The intersection between curriculum and assessment data becomes crucial to these conversations so that they are not based on anecdotes and individual beliefs. Rather, they are focused on what the data tells the group and what additional information they might need to have a more complete picture.

The following are examples of how school leaders have found time to make data analysis possible.

Karen Budan, former assistant superintendent in Glendale Schools and presently the National Director of Professional Services for Performance Pathways, provided time incentives in Glendale in this way:

- We had PD days built into the calendar. I required a certain number to be used for mapping activities such as training and read-throughs.
- We went to our community and asked to be able to add 15 minutes to four days of the week and send the kids home two hours early the fifth day to focus on student achievement. The community agreed and asked we do it on Friday afternoons. So we had two hours every Friday afternoon for school improvement, PD, and mapping activities.

T. C. Boegly, elementary school principal at Colonial School in Plymouth, Pennsylvania, finds that creative scheduling works. Here is one of the ways that she provides time for teachers to analyze data reports from data analysis programs being used by her district:

- At the end of the day for 45 minutes, I create a schedule where a cluster of teachers from a grade level are free so they can collaboratively analyze the assessment data from their benchmark assessments. The students from those classes are sent to other teachers' classrooms where they double-up and have activities for the students until dismissal time.
- The school secretary spends some of her time printing the appropriate reports for the teachers so they can use their time most effectively to focus on instruction.

NEW ROLES FOR TEACHERS AS INCENTIVE

As schools become more organized for the work of mapping and data analysis, teachers are appointed to take on leadership roles to further the work. Formalizing these roles has served as an incentive and serves as leverage in transforming the culture where distributed leadership becomes real. Here are some samples of the types of roles that have been effective.

Teaching and Learning Councils in a Building

Many principals find it important to develop councils that help to guide the initiative. Often, the incentive for being on the council is to be given time to put their attention to meetings. Principals provide substitutes for teachers so they can be relieved of classroom duties in order to attend such meetings. The council generally guides the process for professional development in the building, as well as monitors the process and attends to problems that arise. The council also identifies targeted areas for mapping and assessment analysis.

Subject Area Coaches

Some schools have identified subject area coaches who work with teachers based on assessment data. So, for example, a literacy coach at Furr High School meets with the English department and they analyze the data from the benchmark and state assessments. She helps the teachers integrate new strategies focused on literacy. In addition to her work with the English department, she is also assigned the responsibility of working with the core academic content areas. She demonstrates how to incorporate key strategies to improve student literacy such as vocabulary or note taking. The person in this position is relieved from most of her classroom teaching and is salaried for this new position.

Data Miners

Another interesting new role has been that of the data miner—a person who really likes studying data and is interested in helping others become more proficient at data analysis. In one school, a teacher with these inclinations has been given a stipend to lead his department in this exercise. He provides reports from the mapping program and facilitates the discussion about how those reports can be interpreted. His more sophisticated knowledge about the data helps teachers think more analytically rather than reacting immediately. He presses the discussion to look for root causes that might be affecting the data to identify the difference between a single numerical figure and a pattern within the data. The closer analysis of data has provided a framework for teachers to consider more than one source in order to make decisions.

Data-Informed Facilitators

These teachers are trained and have become skillful at facilitating faculty conversations that lead to important decisions. For many of these teachers, the incentive has been further training and an opportunity for growth. Some may be considering administration at some point in their career and see this as an opportunity to develop new and important skills.

Mapping Coaches

Some schools have designated coaches who are comfortable with technology and curriculum mapping. These teachers are given release time from their classrooms so they can work with their colleagues. Upon request, they can also offer short workshops at a faculty meeting or after school.

Many of the above positions can be formalized in the teacher contract. In that way, union leaders are included in the considerations for building teacher leadership in the organizations. One powerful example of such a contract was designed by Franz Wolff, formerly a teacher and union leader.

Franz secured the proper conditions for teachers by putting the agreements in the union contract. He realized that professional development was central to a teacher's continuous learning. Therefore, he negotiated a process for allocating the professional development budget. The contract specified:

- There would be a professional development committee in every building. The committee would include teachers and administrators, each having only one vote.
- The committee would address the needs of the building and manage the resources they had available, including the budget.

After a successful implementation of the professional development committees, the next negotiation became more specific. The union leaders met and brainstormed what they felt were the educational needs of the teachers. As representatives, they had considerable knowledge about what teachers were discussing and what educational concerns they had. After studying the list, they realized that curriculum was a central concern. In the next contract, they negotiated that there be a district committee to study and gather as much information about curriculum mapping as possible. A few of the schools had already been mapping and they felt that mapping would answer many of their questions about consistency and coherence of curriculum. The committee would include teacher representatives and administrators from each building. In addition, they had the support of the board president, the superintendent, and the director of curriculum for the district.

The combination of the union valuing mapping, the key central administrators valuing mapping, and the distributed leadership among teachers led to a successful enterprise. Key to the success was recognition of the amount of work that needed to be done. Each building was able to develop a plan and use their professional development resources to implement the plan.

Karen Wagner, Middle School Principal, Belle Fourche School District, Belle Fourche, South Dakota, negotiated stipends for her teachers in this way:

> We pay stipends to lead teachers within each building to provide leadership, training, and support to our staff in the mapping process. For teachers, we have 6.5 professional development days scheduled throughout the year. We use three per year where the staff works extra time after school or on Fridays that are off on mapping or other topic-specific professional development activities. One professional development day equals 6.5 hours that they must put in on their own. We keep a log of individual staff hours and they do not have to come in on the regularly scheduled day during the calendar year. By the end of the year they MUST have all their hours recorded or they will receive a pay deduction. The rationale for this approach is to have more consistent work on mapping throughout the year instead of working once for a day in September and then the staff must wait until November or December before the next professional development day is scheduled.

SUMMARY

Transforming a culture challenges all who are complacent to the habits of the existing culture. We have identified two key incentives that help to re-examine the habits of the culture: the way that time is used and the way that teacher roles are defined. Research shows that student achievement is more likely to improve when teachers are directly involved and are taking a leadership role in defining where, when, and how that improvement will be realized (Newmann & Wehlage, 1995; Silns & Mulford, 2002; Spillane, Halverson, & Diamond, 2001). The examples we have selected are few among many that are being enacted across the nation. In each instance, they have served to inspire a change in the way the culture behaves with regard to the collection and analysis of data that impacts the decision-making process.

3 The Intersection of Curriculum and Assessment

In Chapter 1, we developed a vision for the data-informed culture. In Chapter 2, we considered how incentives serve as a significant way to help transform the culture. The question we raise in this chapter is how to begin intersecting curriculum and assessment data. Our vision statement has two critical pathways that serve as a foundation leading to a data-informed culture. One is that of assessment data directly tied to standards, and the second is that of curriculum data tied to standards. Since standards is the common currency upon which decisions will be measured against, we will first discuss how to break the standards into the specific content and skills that are embedded in the standard statement. Next, we will examine how the skills and content become common, intersecting points for ongoing curriculum and assessment development.

CREATING THE STANDARDS-BASED SCHOOL SYSTEM

When using curriculum or assessment data, you must be certain that it is aligned to academic standards. However, as a prelude to this alignment, there must be a real commitment to the meaning of the standards so that all in the community believe that adhering to the standards really describes the appropriate path for a well-educated student. Too often, a district will "drive by" the standard, listing many standards that might be addressed. However, aligning to standards means that there will be a serious focus and intention for instruction and assessment to target that particular standard. Therefore, the standards addressed in curriculum should maintain that same focus. For example, consider the following standard:

> Represent fractions, decimals, percentages, exponents, and scientific notation in equivalent forms.

Stakeholders must ask, "What precisely is expected of the student as a specific learning objective or for a specific test item?"

Educators in South Dakota unpacked all of their English Language Arts (ELA) and science standards so that they would have a more specific description of what is to be learned and what will be tested. Table 3.1 provides an example. The left column shows the wording from the standards document. In the right column, we offer our commentary.

Table 3.1   Unpacked Standard

Standard 3.R.4.1 (Application) **Gather information** *to* **research** *a topic.*	
Verbs Defined: – Gather/collect – Research/find out about	*Notice how they took the key verb in this standard and identified the level of thinking required based on Bloom's taxonomy (Application). In a curriculum map, these verbs would be identified as skills.*
Key Term: – Information – printed text: almanac, atlas, Web site, map, CD-ROM, traditional encyclopedia	*The key terms represent the content in a map.*
Teacher Speak: Students are able to gather *(collect)* information *(printed text)* to research *(find out about)* a topic.	*This helps a teacher identify the learning objectives for this standard.*
Student Speak: I can collect *(gather)* printed text *(information)*—almanac, atlas, Web site, map, CD-ROM, traditional encyclopedia—to find out about *(research)* a topic.	*This transforms the objective into enabling language for students so that it is clear what the learning target is.*

© Performance Pathways. Used with permission.

In order for the system to be standards-based, there must be both internal and external alignment to the standards. Internal alignment refers to map alignment of elements to each other—Essential Questions, Content, Skills, Assessments, and Lessons should all be aligned to one another. Most districts align using the assessments as the basis for alignment. The targets for assessment are clearly identified (Stiggins, 2001) and the essential questions, content, skills, and lessons in the map should be aligned to the assessment. External alignment means that all of the mapping elements (such as content and skills) must also align to the standard. In order to break old habits of working from lessons to standards, many teachers are able to align more easily when they start with the standard, unpack its meaning, identify the content and skills that they will be addressing to help students meet the standard, design assessments that target the standard, and then build the unit of study.

Curriculum and assessment data comes from many levels of the organization. Each level needs to be included in data analysis. We will start by examining the individual classroom level, move to the building level, and finally to the system as a whole. Too often, data is viewed only from the system level and does not learn from the variances that take place at the building and/or classroom level. It is important to understand the multiple perspectives before making decisions that may be appropriate at one level and have too great an impact on another level. We will first examine assessment and then curriculum.

ASSESSMENT DATA: INDIVIDUAL CLASSROOM

Data regarding assessment can be found in a curriculum map. The listing is usually referred to as assessment types. Teachers list the type of assessment used to measure performance. This allows for an analysis of the types of assessments that students have been exposed to. The goal is to provide a well-balanced set of opportunities for students to demonstrate their learning. For example, Table 3.2 shows a breakdown of the number and types of assessments given in Math Pre-Calculus.

Table 3.2   Course: Pre-Calculus Frequency Chart
of the Range of Assessments

Assessment Type	Frequency	Total Assessments in Course	Percent
Constructed Response	18	33	54.55%
Content Based Quiz	18	33	54.55%
Models	4	33	12.12%
Multiple Choice Test	18	33	54.55%
Poster	2	33	6.06%
Simple Research Report	2	33	6.06%
Written Expression	4	33	12.12%

As is apparent, the more precise the information about assessment types, the better the data will be when considering what will be in the best interest of learning about students through classroom-based performance measures. In order to understand what is behind these assessments, educators consider the following questions:

- Is the assessment targeted to the content and skills in the map?
- Is the assessment targeted as a measure of one or more of the standards?
- Is there a good balance of opportunities for students to demonstrate their understanding?

Table 3.3 serves as a guide for examining whether there is a good match between the type of assessment that has been developed and the targets that are represented in content and skills. Each of the methods has types of assessments listed in the cells that correlate with the method. This chart helps a teacher gain clarity about what the targets are, based on standards, and whether the type of assessment is in fact appropriately able to provide information about student learning with regard to those targets.

Table 3.3   Matching Achievement Targets to Assessment Methods

Target to be Assessed	Assessment Method			
	Selected Response Short Answer	Extended Written Response	Performance Assessment	Personal Communication
Knowledge Mastery	Multiple choice, true/false, matching, and fill-in can sample mastery of elements of knowledge; Constructed written response	Exercises can tap understanding of relationships among elements of knowledge	Not a good choice for this target—three other options preferred; Observation	Can ask questions, evaluate answers, and infer mastery, but a time-consuming option; Interview
Reasoning Proficiency	Can assess application of some patterns of reasoning; Multiple choice; Constructed written response	Written descriptions of complex problem solutions can provide a window into reasoning proficiency; Persuasive essay; Analytical essay; Criticism; Descriptive essay	Can watch students solve some problems or examine some products and infer about reasoning proficiency; Observation; Comparative observation	Can ask student to "think aloud" or can ask follow up questions to probe reasoning; Interview; Personal essay
Skills	Can assess mastery of the knowledge prerequisites to skillful performance, but cannot rely on these to tap the skill itself		Can observe and evaluate skills as they are being performed; Observation; Debate; Forum; Choreography	Strong match when skill is oral communication proficiency; also can assess mastery of knowledge prerequisite to skillful performance; Interview
Ability to Create Products	Can assess mastery of the knowledge prerequisite to the ability to create quality products, but cannot use these to assess the quality of products themselves; Descriptive essay; Personal essay; Reflective essay		Can assess proficiency in carrying out steps in product development, and attributes of the product itself; Observation	Can probe procedural knowledge and knowledge of attributes of quality products, but no quality product; Interview
Dispositions	Selected response questionnaire items can tap student feelings	Open-ended questionnaire items can probe dispositions	Can infer dispositions from behavior and products; Observation	Can talk with students about their feelings; Interview

From Rick Stiggins, *Student-Involved Classroom Assessment*, (3rd ed.), © 2001, p. 93, (Table 4.1) with some additions from Bena Kallick. Reprinted by permission of Pearson Education, Inc., Upper Saddle River, NJ.

Information about student learning is critical to improving student achievement. However, data from the classroom is, by necessity, most responsive to the students and their individual needs. For that reason, classroom assessments are often used as assessments *for* learning. Students receive the results of the assessments in a timely fashion and are able to work, with coaching support, to gain specific knowledge about where they need to improve. Although classroom teachers are becoming more precise about the design of their classroom assessments, the results from the classroom must be analyzed in relation to assessments that have been designed for consistency across classrooms. These assessments are commonly known as benchmark assessments.

ASSESSMENT DATA: BENCHMARKS ACROSS GRADES OR COURSES

Many systems are now using benchmark assessments so that there is consistent information across the system about how well prepared students might be for a "high stakes" test. Teachers often participate in the design of these tests, which serves as an excellent professional development experience. When teachers are developing such tests, they become more familiar with the standards and with the curriculum requirements to meet the standards. However, there are often release items from the states that can serve as good test items in addition to many standards-based commercial sources. The critical part of the design of these tests is to make certain that the curriculum is in concert with the test. The following are some considerations:

- The test item should be designed with a discrete indication of the level it is addressing in Bloom's taxonomy.
- The test item is designed to parallel the way the state test is formatted, using comparable language. (Often the students cannot understand the vocabulary or are not familiar with the form in which the test item is presented.)
- A decision needs to be made about whether the test will only address, for example, each quarter of the curriculum, whether it will be cumulative, or whether students will take the entire test each time. This decision should be influenced by how teachers will make use of the results from the test. For example, will teachers be coaching for learning? If so, then the results of the test should be made immediately accessible to both teachers and students. Will the teachers be differentiating the class so that those students who are able to answer questions in advance of the taught curriculum can be given a more challenging curriculum? If so, then giving the whole test each quarter can

serve as a pre-test for some of the curriculum. Will the teacher use the test as a method for spiraling the curriculum, looking to see what is retained over time? If so, then the test should be cumulative.

- Once the test results are accessible, teachers should be meeting at grade or course level to consider any curriculum or instruction decisions that might need to be made to accommodate for student learning. For example, notice in Figure 3.1 that for question number 2, "A" was correct. However, students were distracted by the other options and a low percentage of students identified the correct answer. Was this a problem with the construct of the question? Was this a problem with the way students understood the concept? Is there a need to re-teach this concept? Many teachers will interview a few students to find out what the issue might be. Although a careful analysis of this data is not always possible, when a department or grade-level group does meet together for this sort of conversation, the outcome is most often new knowledge about teaching and learning. When this happens, the professional culture is energized by the data.

Figure 3.1　　Item Analysis Report

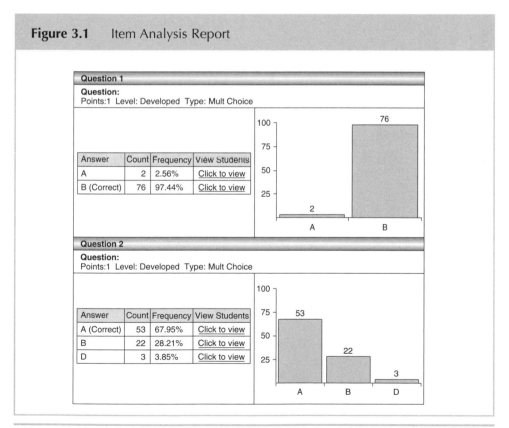

ASSESSMENT DATA: STATE RESULTS

When the data from the classroom and the benchmarks is managed thoughtfully, the state data has more meaning. In one sense, it is an affirmation that the district is staying on the path for improving student learning. In another sense, it can provide a complement to what the district already knows and help the district revisit its assumptions about student learning. In any case, it should not be the final and single point of reference.

Too often state data is presented as a set of numbers. This is what we would call the data. When the numbers are transformed into patterns or trends, we refer to these reports as information. When educators give meaning to the patterns and trends, there is the construction of meaning and the potential for new knowledge about teaching and learning. So, for example, in Figure 3.2 we can see the potential for some powerful system-level conversations about the comparison of performance on the benchmark assessment (4Sight, a state benchmark assessment) in relation to the state performance (PSSA, Pennsylvania State Assessment):

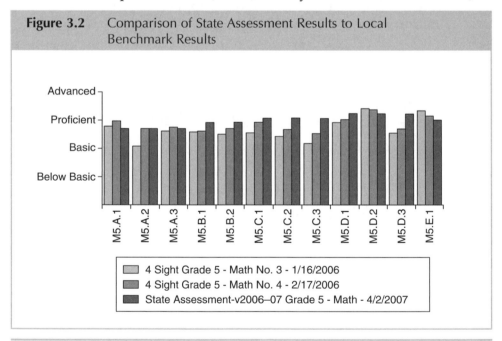

Figure 3.2 Comparison of State Assessment Results to Local Benchmark Results

© Performance Pathways. Used with permission.

CURRICULUM DATA: INDIVIDUAL CLASSROOM LEVEL

A teacher can review his map to make certain that it is well aligned with standards. Once again, a summary of what is in the map is very helpful.

Since most teachers are using a landscape version of the map (most typically using mapping software), they are able to see a year at a glance by scrolling down through each map. Teachers diary maps are based on what is taking place in the classroom. When using technology, they are able to modify in response to their students' learning. They are able to see what standards they have addressed and how frequently. They can also see which standards have not been addressed. Maps serve as a tool for inquiry and self-reflection. Maps are often a part of a teacher's portfolio. As a teacher studies her maps over time, she can see her own growth as a teacher.

CURRICULUM DATA: ACROSS AND WITHIN COURSE OR GRADE LEVEL

As mapping data is collected, a read through (Jacobs, 1997) process occurs. Teachers use the data from their maps to have both mixed and grade-level reviews. Once teachers converse with one another about what is in their maps, they realize the significance of mapping. They search for gaps and repetitions. They learn what is happening at another developmental level for students. They gain new insights about their own work as well as the work of others. They are able to serve as critical friends to one another, making certain that standards alignment is real and realistic.

THE INTERSECTION OF CURRICULUM MAPPING AND ASSESSMENT

The following provides a continuum for system-level self-assessment. This continuum is designed to bring together the significant dimensions for a district: curriculum mapping, assessment, professional learning community, and the use of technology. Each dimension of the continuum contributes to the whole of the vision. It is designed as a continuum rather than a rubric, meaning that it is understood that transforming the culture is a process that will take place over time. The statement of development along the continuum moves through the following dimensions:

- Initial status: Where is the district at this time with regard to this dimension?
- Prologue: Where is the district in preparing for the changes that will be taking place?
- Getting started: Where is the district in starting the initiative?
- Advanced mapping: Where is the district in advancing the initiative? How much further along is the district since initial implementation?

- Organizational process established: Note that this is a continuum and the end goal is that there is a process established for sustaining all of the dimensions. Ultimately, when all processes are established, there will be a transformation of the culture. When new people enter the culture, it will be understood that "this is the way we do business here."

Many districts use this as the basis for setting up their action plan as well as measuring how well they are doing as they lead the district to becoming a data-informed culture.

Table 3.4   Continuum for System-Level Self-Assessment

	1 Initial Status	*2 Prologue*
Curriculum and Instruction	Curriculum guides are updated infrequently. There is little or no collection of evidence regarding what is actually taught in classrooms. Curriculum committees or central administrators make decisions about curriculum revision.	Mapping information is considered. Teachers and administrators study mapping and determine what their purpose would be for mapping. TechPaths is selected as the tool for managing curriculum, instruction, and assessment.
Assessment	Assessment data is analyzed by central administrators. Teachers do not do much data analysis based on classroom results as well as benchmark and state results.	Teachers see models of assessment data and how it is used for effective teaching innovations. Teachers begin to identify professional development needs with regard to building high quality assessments in their classrooms.
Professional Community for Learning	Teachers tend to either be isolated in their practices or meet only within their grades or courses. The general mode is: "close my door and do my thing."	Teachers are exposed to research about professional learning communities. The first learning community is established as a study group to practice being a group that is focused on teaching and learning.
Use of Technology	Teachers do not use technology for managing curriculum. There is no integrated approach for the organization of curriculum, instruction, or assessment data.	Teachers attend training sessions on technology. Teachers understand the possibilities that technology offers in terms of a shared, relational data base.
	3 Getting Started	*4 Advanced Mapping*
Curriculum and Instruction	Teachers are introduced to mapping concepts and TechPaths technology. Initial data entry begins. The first read-through of data from curriculum maps takes place. Initial revision of curriculum.	Read-through of maps leads to professional development needs. Schools address instructional needs based on the quality of the units and their alignment, as well as the quality of the classroom-based assessments. Maps are continuously revised based on new learning.
Assessment	Professional development focuses on how to build high quality assessments in the classroom. System develops high quality benchmark assessments. Data is tracked and informational reports are made available to teachers for analysis and decision-making.	Assessment practices interact with curriculum and instruction. Decisions are made on the basis of high quality data both in maps and in assessment results.

(continued)

Table 3.4   Continuum for System-Level Self-Assessment (continued)

	3 Getting Started	4 Advanced Mapping
Professional Community for Learning	Teachers become part of the planning process. Councils for teaching and learning are established in the buildings and at the central level. Teacher leadership is recognized with some form of incentive. Learning communities reach beyond the school or district and learn from the TechPaths world wide search, as well as conferences that are planned to foster networking around high quality maps, units, content, skills, assessments, and lessons.	Many teachers have the capacity for facilitating groups and shepherding the process of studying curriculum, instruction, and assessment. Curriculum decisions are made through a collaborative process. Timelines are met and the community maintains high standards for itself as well as for students.
Use of Technology	Teachers enter mapping data into the software. They are able to use the search feature and are beginning to use reports on standards addressed, assessment types, this unit detailed, and landscape versions. Teachers are using the world wide search for innovations from other schools in the technology community.	Teachers are facile with the technology and know how to enter lessons and assessments associated with units of study. They are able to use all of the reports and are meeting with others on the basis of the data in the reports.
Organizational Process Established		
Curriculum and Instruction	Mapping is used as the tool for organizing, reviewing, and revising curriculum based on assessment data. Curriculum is aligned to standards and is also aligned according to essential questions, content, skills, assessments, and lessons. There is a system for identifying quality maps, units, lessons, and assessments based on student learning. All teachers use mapping tool for planning and documenting practice.	
Assessment	Assessment data drives changes in curriculum and instruction. There is a system for analyzing assessment and curriculum data in order to make revisions.	
Professional Community for Learning	Teachers share data, analyze curriculum, instruction, and assessment. Self-directed learning groups take leadership in learning and innovating on behalf of student learning.	
Use of Technology	The technology is a tool for managing all lessons, assessments, and curriculum. The system is using the reports for all read-through processes. The data from the reports serves as a basis for data driven decision-making.	

SUMMARY

Transformation of the culture requires clarity, process, and action. Although we hear the phrase "data-driven decision making," we often do not see clearly what is meant by data. We have described data from the perspective of the classroom, building, and system. In addition, we have provided a continuum that will help a district determine where it is in the change process and what actions may need to take place in order to continue improving student achievement. In Chapter 4, we will focus on how the use of protocols provides a facilitation process for new ways of leading with data.

4 Leading With Data

Whether the vision lives or dies can be attributed directly to the leadership within a district. If we are concerned with not only introducing but also sustaining the vision, we must make certain that the leadership understands, supports, and gains strength from the use of data throughout the district.

Because so much data can exist in any district, it is important to set realistic expectations regarding the use of that data. When beginning, try to identify and focus initially on specific data and the appropriate use of that data. Given constraints of time and resources, more data is not necessarily better, and quantity does not necessarily guarantee quality. A common model we use when beginning to facilitate data dialogue is to start with just the following key data:

- Performance results from state tests aligned to current state standards
- Performance results from local benchmarks aligned to the same standards
- Curriculum aligned to standards
- Classroom-based lesson plans and assessments

Time for meetings is limited and must be focused. We suggest that using protocols can serve to facilitate a meeting efficiently. Many people refer to these protocols as "tuning protocols." Tuning refers to the way you tune in to a radio station, making certain that you are in exactly the right frequency so that you have eliminated all static. Likewise, when working with a group, you want to make certain that the group members are all attuned to one another and that static is eliminated. This does not mean that there cannot be disagreements or discord. In fact, the group needs to learn how to have real dialogue—not false harmony. A protocol simply provides agenda facilitation so that all members of the group are clear about the time they will spend on each part of the protocol as well as the process that they are participating in.

The following are some tips to guide group dialogue:

- Make certain that you have the right people at the table. Any curriculum or assessment for eleven-year-olds is basically a cumulative result of work done with eight-, nine-, ten-, and eleven-year-olds. Therefore, you need to have representation from mixed year levels of study.
- Don't react quickly to the data. Use the data as the basis for inquiry rather than as jumping to actions or conclusions.
- Establish group norms for behavior. For example, many people use the following norms when starting group work (Costa & Kallick, 2000):

  1. Listening with understanding and empathy: Listen first to understand what another person is saying before trying to say what is on your mind.
  2. Managing impulsivity: Resist jumping to conclusions or accusations. Stop and think about what the data might be saying.
  3. Questioning and problem posing: Look for patterns and trends in the data. Raise questions. Use data as an opportunity for inquiry before decision-making.

USING STATE ASSESSMENT DATA

Due to No Child Left Behind and raised levels of accountability, this data often causes the greatest degree of dialogue. Districts often take the position that the data does not have credibility because it is not matched with their daily instruction. Details lacking an explanation of the alignment to standards and formulae related to proficiency levels further the question of credibility. In our work, State Assessment Data is best used to set targets, and develop a model using actions and timelines to monitor progress against strategic goals. The data that we receive from these tests usually comes too late with too little specific information to be used solely to impact and revise instruction.

When reviewing state assessment results, also study your curriculum data. In order to know how to address any issues in your data, you need to also know what is being taught in the schools. Curriculum mapping is significant data because it reflects what is actually being taught in your classrooms. With the advent of currently available technologies, a district is now able to transform curriculum that used to be in a text-bound guide to actual living data. For example, the data can transform text to quantifiable terms so that you can see a frequency count of where the information is being taught, when it is being taught, and to what degree it is being assessed. You can see this data from the perspective of the individual classroom through to the building and out to all classes in the district. Curriculum mapping, when used in conjunction with technology, can provide additional significant information about how to address your performance results.

A Protocol for Studying State Assessment Data

English Mathematics Achievement
Analysis Making Predictions

Where do you think your students did particularly well?
This is a particularly good strategy for reading the data purposefully. If teachers predict before they look at the data they (a) are then eager to affirm or disaffirm their predictions so they enter the analysis with a question and (b) may find their biases have affected their expectations for students. We look at the results from common benchmark assessments as the basis for making predictions (see Figure 4.1).

Where do you think they may not have performed particularly well?
Considering this question provides time for the teacher to also reflect on where the emphasis for instruction has been and why those decisions were made.

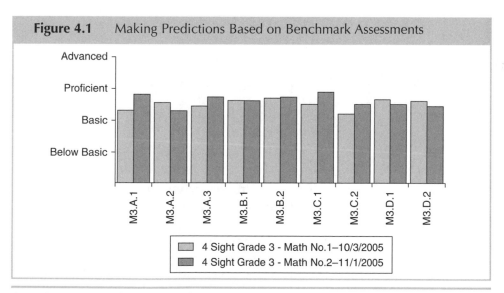

Figure 4.1 Making Predictions Based on Benchmark Assessments

© Performance Pathways. Used with permission.

Once teachers have made their predictions, they compare those predictions to the actual performance. They are able to look at both the benchmark assessments and the state assessments so that they are able to compare both their own predictions and determine how well the benchmarks serve as a good measure for anticipating how students will perform on the state assessments. This work provides a level of analysis that asks teachers to re-examine their benchmarks as well as consider what interventions they might have used to improve performance for the students.

Figure 4.2   Compare to Actual Performance

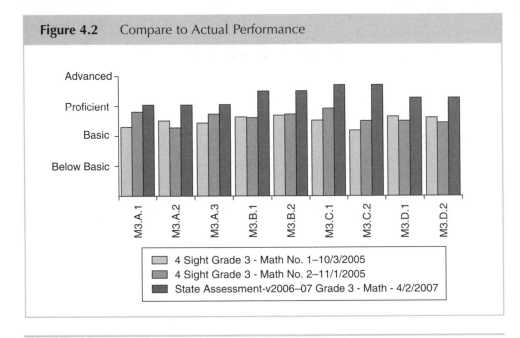

4 Sight Grade 3 - Math No. 1–10/3/2005
4 Sight Grade 3 - Math No. 2–11/1/2005
State Assessment-v2006–07 Grade 3 - Math - 4/2/2007

© Performance Pathways. Used with permission.

COMPARING STATE RESULTS AND CURRICULUM MAPPING DATA

Areas of Strength

- Identify and list in Table 4.1 an area where you predicted that students would do well and where your prediction matched the actual outcomes.
- Go to the set of curriculum maps and study the pattern of instruction around that area. Be certain that you review at least two grades that preceded the grade-level test results that you are studying.
- What did you notice about the taught curriculum in those areas?
- Are there any patterns that you observe?

Areas of Possible Concern

- Identify an area where students are not performing especially well. You may want to choose an area where your predictions did not match the state results.
- Go to your curriculum maps and study the pattern of instruction around that area. Be sure to look at two grade levels that precede the grade-level test results that you are studying.
- What did you notice about the taught curriculum in that area?
- Are there any patterns that you observe?

Table 4.1   Prioritizing and Developing Strategies to Address the Areas of Concern

Area of Concern	Strategy to Address	How curriculum mapping and benchmark assessments can help to address the area of concern
1.		
2.		
3.		
4		
5.		
6.		
Other Factors to Consider When Analyzing the Test and Mapping Data		

PERFORMANCE DATA FROM LOCAL BENCHMARK ASSESSMENTS

Local, standards-based benchmark assessments are a powerful tool that can be used to monitor the progress of performance-based goals. We obviously have to be cognizant of the validity and alignment to standards for these assessments, but because districts have much more control and flexibility of the design and content within their local assessments, the data is typically more readily accepted. In addition, when using the proper technologies, results can be timely and can therefore be used immediately to impact instruction. This data is likely to have far greater implications for the daily lives of students in the classroom. Here are some guidelines for local benchmark assessments:

- The quality of the results depends on the quality of the test items.
- Aligning each item to standards is critical.
- Designing each assessment to measure longitudinal progress of all the standards provides clearly measured progress against goals.
- Making certain that the timing of the benchmarks is in concert with the timing of the curriculum.
- Looking at the scope and sequence of your curriculum data in relation to the timing of the local assessment will help to give you a better picture of how teachers are covering the curriculum, how they are sequencing their instruction, and how well prepared you can assume students will be for the particular items in the benchmark assessments.

PROTOCOL FOR ANALYZING BENCHMARK ASSESSMENTS AND MAPS

Working in critical friends groups (no larger than four to a group), analyze the results from the benchmark assessment using the following questions:

- What were the assessment targets? Did the targets match up with the content and skills that are in the maps for this period of time?
- Should the assessment be a measure of what we have taught so far, as well as a guide to measure how far we are from our final destination?
- Did we have the appropriate assessment method to get at the content and skills targets that we identified?

CLASSROOM DATA

A key point we learned from our work with continuous improvement is that the quality of the work rests in the hands of the worker. All achievement depends on students caring about their performance and wanting to improve. Teachers often feel that their classroom assessments hold better credibility for both instruction and for student feedback than do any more occasional tests, such as the ones above. It is in the classroom that teachers are able to coach, instruct, provide rich feedback, and most significantly, help students to become more self-assessing.

Here are some tips for classroom-based assessments:

- The quality of these assessments depends on a teacher's understanding about how to design good assessments. They need to know how to choose the appropriate method for assessment, such as constructed response, multiple choice, and performance assessment. The method is determined by the assessment targets—what is it that you want the students to demonstrate in this assessment?
- This is a place where year level meetings can be very productive, especially for design work. However, the design is only as good as the product that results. Time for teachers to talk about student work, analyzing the results, and understanding more about how to coach students for improved performance is essential.

PROTOCOL FOR ANALYZING STUDENT WORK IN RELATION TO THEIR MAPS

A small group of teachers each have a copy of a particular piece of work that a student has generated. The presenter of the work describes what the work was targeting. In addition, the presenter provides the curriculum map that is associated with the work.

- Round One: The teachers describe what they see in the work. It is important to only describe what you see and not infer what is not there. This round provides an opportunity to really hear the student voice in the work without filtering it with teacher expectations. Each teacher contributes one thing that they see and the group goes around until there is nothing left to add.
- Round Two: What questions arise for you as you considered the work and the curriculum map?
- Round Three: What do we need to consider as we reflect on what we have learned in this discussion?

CURRICULUM MAPPING DATA

As has been suggested in analyzing the assessment data, it all leads back to curriculum and instruction. Sometimes the questions are at the individual classroom level: What can I do to more effectively address the needs of my students this year? Sometimes they come at the school level: How can we make certain that we are all providing the most consistent use of language, vocabulary, and strategies for learning so that students can become more successful? Sometimes they come at the department level: Do we have too many repetitions in our curriculum? Does the curriculum spiral and increase in complexity? What needs to be more important? Less important? What might need to be dropped?

PROTOCOL FOR CHECKING THE QUALITY OF THE MAP

Purpose of this check:

- To make certain that the map is clear to a reader who may not be familiar with the course of study that is represented, and
- To make certain that there is alignment among the elements of the maps (Essential Questions, Content, Skills, Assessments).

This protocol is often used before teachers participate in a read-through process in which they will be making decisions regarding curriculum revision. It is a variation on a consultation protocol in which group members consult with one another in order to elevate the quality of their work. These groups usually take place either during a faculty meeting in a building or as part of a professional development day in the district.

Stage One (15 minutes)

Each individual teacher checks the quality of his or her own map against the checklist below. This offers the teacher an opportunity to reflect on the map and make adjustments and revisions.

Is there alignment between:

- Essential Questions
- Detail on Content
- Precise Skills
- Targeted Assessments
- Standards

Stage Two (1 hour)

Once teachers have checked their own maps for quality, they are set up in a critical friends group that is comprised of mixed disciplines and grades. It is useful to keep the group size to three for this protocol. This would allow for each of the group members to have a round of presentation.

These groups are referred to as vertical groups and they are especially productive because they allow teachers to have a systems view of curriculum and assessment.

- Critical friends each receive a copy of the map from each member of the group.
- Each presents their own map to the group. The following is the protocol to be used by the group:

Each presenter has 20 minutes.

Review and Clarifying Questions (8 minutes)

Review the map using the same checklist for alignment as above. Group starts by using clarifying questions. If there is anything in the map that is not clear to the reader, the person asks the presenter to clarify. For example, a question might be asked such as, "I notice that your assessment type is a quiz and that your content lists very complex ideas. Can you help me understand how the quiz is aligned to the content?"

Question From the Presenter (3 minutes)

The presenter, after answering questions of clarification, might raise a question that he or she would like the group to consider. For example, the presenter might be stimulated by the question of assessment type and may ask, "Given what I have just observed about my map, I am wondering if the group can help me know how to make certain that my assessment types are, in fact, better aligned with content."

Group Interacts (9 minutes)

There is time for the group to engage with the question and work on behalf of the presenter. The presenter summarizes the discussion and what has been learned.

CURRICULUM DIALOGUE

In Pelham, New York, they are developing the intersection of curriculum mapping and assessment by (a) developing consensus maps and (b) developing local benchmark assessments. The following is a statement of their purpose and a protocol for the second year of realizing their vision to become "data smart" (they are using the term S.M.A.R.T. with reference to making SMART goals that are specific, measurable, attainable, realistic, and timely as described in Chapter 1) as a culture. This text is part of a script that the curriculum coaches will be using when they present the protocol for building consensus. In this district, they have assigned time for curriculum dialogue. They will be using this protocol in that time.

PROTOCOL FOR CURRICULUM DIALOGUE

This year we will be attuning our curriculum maps and benchmark assessments to New York State standards. Although teachers individually plan many powerful classroom-based experiences, in order for us to become "data smart" we need to make certain that we share some comparable measures to inform our decisions about curriculum and assessment. The comparable measures are based on New York State standards. When we are measuring against standards, we are ascertaining whether:

- Our curriculum is designed to maximize the possibility that all students will achieve performance as indicated in the standard,
- Our assessment measures are well aligned with the standards so that they can serve as credible evidence,
- Students have the opportunity to perform to the standards given multiple measures rather than limiting assessment to one method, and
- Students receive feedback about their performance as they progress so that they are clear about how to improve.

Two of our most significant sources for this data about student learning come from our curriculum maps and our benchmark assessments. The consensus maps that we developed last year suggest a curriculum that all students will address. We expect that teachers will honestly modify the core curriculum as is necessary to respond to students. These modifications should be recorded in your curriculum maps so that we have accurate data about what was actually addressed. Revisions of curriculum will be informed by the information from these documents. The benchmark assessments represent assessments that all students will be given the opportunity to perform.

As we study the data from both maps and assessments sources, we will be able to focus on whether students performed to the standard and at what level of proficiency. We will be able to study the curriculum maps to know how the standards were addressed—in what year and with what degree of frequency. We will then have the information needed to take action to address student learning needs.

Our ultimate goal will be to modify maps and benchmarks on the basis of what we learn from a year of close examination and reflection. Many of you have asked that we stay with the same goals over time so that we can deepen our knowledge about student performance. The process design for this year is focused on responding to that request.

CONSENSUS MAPPING PROCESS

1. Identify three to five power standards from among the ones you have indicated in your maps to be included on the consensus map. (Look for overlaps of standards to look for clusters of the similar content or skills.)
   [Input agreed-upon standards onto consensus map template. Click "standards alignment." Then choose "Self-Assessment" and in description write "Consensus Map Standards." Check off standards.]
2. Unpack each standard by identifying content (key terms) and skills (verbs) embedded in each standard.

Table 4.2   Example of Unpacking a Standard

NY: Social Studies, NY: Intermediate, History of the US and NY – Consider the sources of historic documents, narratives, or artifacts and evaluate their reliability.	
Key Terms:	Verbs (Skills):
sources	consider
historic documents	evaluate
narratives	
artifacts	
reliability	

© Performance Pathways. Used with permission.

3. Review maps for content and skills covered by unpacked standards.
   [Discuss language of content and skills and then input onto consensus map template.]
4. Identify content and skills *not* stated in standards.
5. Identify *additional* content and skills ALL students should learn.
   [Discuss language of additional content and skills to be included and then input onto consensus map template.]
6. Check essential questions' alignment with standards. Do they guide students' uncovering of important ideas in content? [Discuss language of questions and input agreed-upon questions onto consensus map template.]
7. Note agreed upon content and skills on "Group Meeting Report" sheet.
8. Note content and skills in question on "Group Meeting Report" sheet.
9. Complete the reflective stems on "Group Meeting Report" sheet.
10. Follow same steps for each unit of your consensus map. Each department will meet every last Wednesday of the month to work on a consensus map unit.

SUMMARY

The pathways to success for student achievement require collaborative work among teachers, administrators, and students. The greater the clarity of expectations and well-targeted assessments, the more likely students will be able to participate in the process of learning. The curriculum map can serve as a road map for improvement. As teachers become more skillful analyzing assessment results in relation to their maps, they will also become more skillful conferencing with students to help them become more engaged in the direction of their own learning.

Introduction to Case Studies

Humans are not ideally set up to understand logic; they are ideally set up to understand stories.
—Roger C. Shank, Cognitive Scientist

We have made the case for data as shown in its most logical and understandable form. Most of the work in Chapters 1–4 has been derived from readings and, most importantly, experience in the field. The case studies in Chapters 5–7 present stories from the field that enhanced our understanding of the work. We invited educators from three districts to share their journeys with as much honesty as possible. We suggest the possibility of readers using these stories as an additional form of analysis of our text. You may want to provide some reflective questions to consider after reading each case, such as:

- How well did the authors describe their vision and purpose for the work?
- How did the authors use data to inform their decisions?
- What were some of the struggles in translating their vision into operational terms?
- Identify aspects from each story that resonate with stories from your district. What can you learn from these stories that might help you with your practices?

The West Seneca story was selected to illuminate a journey with curriculum mapping.

Colonial was selected to detail how a district, and then a specific elementary school, learned to use assessment data more powerfully.

West Chester High School is a story of a high school that has successfully brought its faculty to a deeper understanding of its curriculum and assessments through mapping.

5 Case Study 1

West Seneca Central School District

Jeanne Tribuzzi   *Brandon Wiley*
Brian Graham   *Tana Cleveland*

The decision to undertake change more often than not is accompanied by a kind of optimism and rosy view of the future that, temporarily at least, obscures the predictable turmoil ahead. But that turmoil cannot be avoided and how well it is coped with separates the boys from the men, the girls from the women. It is . . . rough stuff . . . . There are breakthroughs, but also brick walls.

—Seymour Sarason

Authors' Note

Case studies provide a rich opportunity to hear, from the voice of the practitioners involved, how some of the work that we are proposing plays out in a district. We selected three case studies, each of which provides a different perspective. In this chapter, we focus on West Seneca Central School District. They have worked deliberately and extensively to use curriculum mapping as a catalyst for developing K–12 consistency and continuity. We intend for these case study chapters to be read with others on your team so that you can consider the questions raised. In this chapter, you might wonder how much of what they describe matches your district. When reading a story from another district, be certain that you remain flexible in your thinking—what works for these people? What would work for us? How might what they have learned help the way we might progress in our own work?

OVERCOMING ROADBLOCKS TO SUCCESS: PERSEVERING TO MAKE CURRICULUM MAPPING WORK

In an age of increasing accountability and high stakes testing, many school districts across the nation are feeling the pressure to improve student achievement like never before. While some have eagerly sought the one "magic bullet" to solve this dilemma, schools that hope to bring about lasting and enduring change need to think systemically. The process of curriculum mapping has the potential to actually bring about that systemic change within a school district. Mapping brings about the opportunity for districts to change the way "they do business" on several levels. By utilizing mapping technology, curriculum mapping allows administrators and teachers to record, analyze, and make important decisions about instruction. It changes the way teachers plan instruction and helps them make more informed decisions regarding what is in the best interest of their students. It allows administrators to operate as instructional leaders within their school and provides greater insight into what is actually taking place in the classroom. Now that mapping can occur via the Internet, it provides teachers an opportunity to articulate and align curriculum, while providing a vehicle for greater communication, collaboration, and coaching even from the comfort of their home computer.

The practice of documenting and analyzing the instruction that takes place within the classroom with technology is still relatively new to education. Curriculum mapping requires a great deal of planning and preparation to ensure that all involved have a clear idea of how the process will work and why it is being done. Setting the stage for a successful implementation is crucial to avoid frustration, confusion, and abandonment of the project.

As of this writing, West Seneca Central School District is in its second year of mapping and we are slowly embedding the process in all curricular and policy areas in the district. This change has not been free of turbulence and frustration because of a less than perfect implementation process. Our story includes some of these frustrations and ways we have been able to persevere to overcome them.

West Seneca Central School District Overview

West Seneca is a large suburban district, with seven elementary schools, two middle schools, two high schools, and an alternative educational center. The district is a first ring suburb of the city of Buffalo, New York, with an enrollment of approximately 7,500 students. An administrative team that consists of 26 building and central office administrators leads a teaching staff of approximately 630 teachers.

The turnover of teachers and administrators in the last several years has been significant in West Seneca. Nearly 200 members of the teaching staff and 17 members of the administrative team are within their first three years in the district. The district prides itself on continually focusing on improved instructional practices, differentiated professional development, and a technological infrastructure that is second to none in the western New York area. An informed and proactive school board has further supported the desire for constant improvement. No Child Left Behind (NCLB) legislation and changes in assessment requirements in New York State indicated that our next focused effort in the district had to take place in the area of curriculum development.

Curriculum and New Teachers

"Will we actually receive a curriculum that tells us what we're supposed to teach through the year?" We can all still remember either hearing or thinking this question during our undergraduate teaching courses. Curriculum is a concept that seems so simple and perfunctory, yet often, existing curriculum in any school district isn't as concise and well articulated as one would think. Some course curricula are easier to define than others, with areas such as elementary language arts being especially challenging.

A preservice teacher may start a teaching career with the idea that the curriculum will be provided for them in a neat document that will be easy to follow. The reality of what most new teachers find when they enter their first classroom is that no such document exists. Once they realize that there may not be much in the way of guidance other than a reading series, they suffer quietly to avoid drawing attention to the fact that they are not quite sure what they should be teaching. They must work to collect, share, search, learn, borrow, copy, integrate, and guess as they determine what to teach the children.

It takes a few years, but an established program of study begins to emerge once a teacher has worked hard to assemble all of the materials and lessons that make up her curriculum. This curriculum is now "owned" by the teacher who created it and the teacher sometimes behaves like a proud parent, sharing stories about the lessons, activities, and successes she is having within the classroom. This may be a wonderful experience for the proud teacher, but the student who lives through 13 years of creative curriculum may not feel the same sense of pride or accomplishment—especially if the student has experienced some of these activities or lessons more than once.

Curriculum in West Seneca

For elementary teachers in the West Seneca school district, working without an articulated language arts curriculum wasn't too unusual. Elementary curriculum in the district was strongly influenced by whatever reading or math series was being used, and teachers filled in the rest of the gaps with materials that either appealed to them or were available to them. We have masterful teachers in West Seneca, but the fact remains that teachers create programs that are somewhat unique to their classroom. This is to be expected; teachers should enrich existing curriculum, but existing curriculum is the key word. The written curriculum in the district was dated and many teachers relied on the reading series to be the curriculum. The master teachers who were able to use quality children's literature to teach students to read and write, while learning about the world, possess skills that take years to develop. With new state standards and federal mandates, the language arts curriculum in the district warranted some examination. We didn't have the time to provide professional development to new teachers to help them create fabulous programs because new assessments were looming around the corner. Despite the fact that reading and writing at the elementary level can be very complex, we began our mapping work in this area because we were lacking a curriculum that was aligned to new performance indicators.

New York State, as a response to NCLB, implemented testing in Grades 3–8, causing greater concern about what we were actually teaching students. While our students had performed fairly well on previous assessments, the new assessments raised the level of expectations and called for greater alignment of curriculum and instruction. The curriculum review process began by bringing together a group of teachers and administrators to align the scope and sequence of the existing reading series and the performance indicators that were being measured on the state tests in Grades 4 and 8.

THE PROLOGUE TO CURRICULUM MAPPING

Several administrators had knowledge of the theory of curriculum mapping and we thought that perhaps a way to address the concerns these teachers raised might be to move our curriculum work in this direction. Several other administrators joined us in this investigation as we put our heads together to share what we knew about Heidi Hayes Jacobs' work in curriculum mapping (1997, 2006) We were eager, excited for a positive change in the curriculum process, and somewhat idealistic. Thus began our curriculum mapping journey.

As a plan began to form, we knew it was important to include input from all of the teachers in the district, based on our limited participation over the summer. A paper template was created that contained what we thought were the essential components of quality English Language Arts (ELA) curriculum. The idea was that we would ask teachers to document what literature they read each month, what content understandings they addressed, what skills they taught, and how they were assessing this learning. We also asked that they include the alignment to the standards. A few of these completed templates are included in the Resources section at the back of this book as Early Curriculum Maps.

The teachers were then asked to send us those completed paper templates, and our job was to consolidate them and tally the number of times a skill, title, or content understanding was taught in a month at each grade level. This took an enormous amount of time and the number of hours we were spending on the process was not conducive to maintaining a life of any kind, either at work or personally. More important, the teachers didn't see the work that was happening on our end until we brought them back to a meeting where we shared this consolidated data. When discussions about this data didn't lead us to any conclusions, and teachers looked at us in bewilderment, we knew again that we had to come up with another plan for curriculum development.

In September 2004, we attended a local conference with our Director of Technology, an elementary principal, and a middle school principal. Dr. Heidi Hayes Jacobs was giving an overview of the mapping process and discussed how to implement mapping in a district. Her logical explanation of the process made it clear that this was the path we needed to follow.

It became obvious to us that we had to use technology to support our mapping initiative and we began the investigation of the curriculum mapping software that was available on the market. After developing a rubric, three different programs were evaluated by a team of administrators and teachers. We selected the program that best met our requirements. While this solved our "paper problem," it created the need to plan how and when we would train our teachers to use the technology. Our mapping initiative was driven by a small leadership team and a representative group of teachers who were filled with trepidation. Table 5.1 shows our first year's plan for a prologue on mapping and getting started with the technology.

Table 5.1   Action Plan, Year One

Year	Key Action	Person Responsible/Involved
Year One 2004–2005	Present curriculum mapping overview to each elementary building faculty	Jeanne Tribuzzi, Brandon Wiley, Mark Beehler
	Create design teams (K–5), one teacher from each grade level per building	Jeanne Tribuzzi, Brandon Wiley, Building principals, (42 teachers K–5), Tribuzzi, Wiley, Beehler, Todorof, B. Graham, Kovach, Board of Cooperative Educational Services (BOCES), & Hamburg reps
	Select curriculum mapping software	All K–5 elementary teachers of ELA
	Diary map ELA content, skills, assessment (K–5)	Design team members, Tribuzzi/Wiley to facilitate
	Design team to meet monthly to refine process, make suggestions for process	Tribuzzi, Beehler, Graham
	"Train the Trainer" workshop w/ H.H. Jacobs, Janet Hale, and Hector Mendez – Palm Springs	Select administrators/teachers CO – 3, WSR – 3, ESR – 5, WM – 6, EM – 6, Elem – 4
	"Train the Trainer" workshop with Janet Hale	Jeanne Tribuzzi, Brandon Wiley
	"Making CM the Hub for School Improvement and Increased Student Performance" ASCD Preconference	All elementary principals, high school principals, district administration
	Training with Janet Hale for building and district administrators	
Summer 2005	Techpaths training for untrained exploratory teachers	Facilitated by Wiley/Tribuzzi Literacy, Reading, Art, Music, Phys. Ed, Enrichment teachers as available
	Techpaths training for secondary teachers	Facilitated by Wiley/Tribuzzi Middle/High school teachers as available
	Continue mapping with Techpaths for elementary teachers – "curriculum writing"	Elementary teachers who have already been trained and are mapping with Techpaths
	Enter "essential" district maps for elementary social studies, math, and science into the system	

LEADERSHIP

Two of us were starting as new administrators at the district level, which provided us with an opportunity to institute change, but also created several challenges. Having both recently left the classroom, we had a keen sense of the realities of teaching elementary and middle school. In the earliest stages of the project, we shared our vision with building principals, with the support of our assistant superintendent for curriculum and instruction. Our ideas were met with approval, but there were other pressing matters to discuss. Instead of taking note of the less than enthusiastic reception to mapping, we plunged ahead. For a period of about a month, we traveled to each elementary building, sharing the vision for curriculum mapping and stating the goals we hoped to accomplish. This small "road show" allowed us to communicate the logic behind mapping and what benefits it would have on instruction and student learning.

What we failed to do was work closely to include the involvement of the building principals and all of the teachers in the development of that vision. Most faculties we spoke to smiled and nodded as we presented. What we had to say made sense to them, but many felt "this too shall pass," like so many other initiatives. The initial input and collaboration with all of the key players in the district was not sufficient when it came to implementing a process that would change much of how we operated. We can honestly say that at this point we did not realize the true magnitude of the work and the systemic change that mapping is leading us to today.

To begin the training on technology, we assembled a representative group of teachers and worked with them in the early stages of the process. This "design team" was created to help us with the initial implementation and training. This group was representative of teachers in Grades K–5, from each grade level and building. We had hoped that this design team would be fairly proficient in mapping and serve as the "go-to" people in their buildings. However, we did not formally recognize them as coaches or mentors. The role they would play as leaders in their buildings was not clearly stated and the expectations from building to building were inconsistent. Many of them were not comfortable serving in a leadership position, largely because they still struggled with the question of why we were mapping. This group of teachers was our communication link to the other teachers, and they often faced unhappy colleagues back in their buildings. This did not boost their enthusiasm for helping to lead this initiative.

In November, we had our initial training on the curriculum mapping software with this design team of approximately 25 teachers. The first critical conversation focused on presenting the basic tenets of mapping and explaining what content, skills, and assessment really meant. In addition to defining each of these elements, we had to deal with some apprehension about the software as the tool we would be using.

Over the course of the school year, the design team met monthly, and continued to enter mapping data and practice the review process. In addition, we began to train all K–5 general education teachers in the buildings using the software. They were given the option to continue mapping on paper or to use the technology. In the first year, over 150 teachers were trained to create diary maps online. Throughout the early training, it was necessary to continually review the vision and goals of the diary mapping process. Some teachers were quick to see the benefits, while others remained skeptical. The monthly meetings with the design team were often emotional and revealed the frustration teachers were experiencing with emerging issues regarding mapping. Teachers felt the expectations were not clear. They also felt that mapping was one more thing on an already "full plate." In each of these meetings and trainings, we invited teachers to voice their concerns. This feedback was critical in helping to make decisions and modify expectations. Most important, it provided a forum for dialogue, allowing us to address specific concerns and issues. It was also the first critical step for us to build trusting relationships with teachers. Overall, it communicated to us that although we thought our vision was clear, perhaps it was only clear to us.

The mapping process continued with growing involvement from the teaching ranks and support from central office and building principals. If the teachers felt their plates were full, the building administrators were managing a daily "buffet" on their plates. By conducting the first round of training without the administrators and working only with teachers in the buildings, we had hoped to alleviate some of the administrative workload. Many administrators were relieved that we were leading the charge and conducting the training in their buildings. In reality, it caused those who were not involved at the initial stages of training to feel ill prepared and uneasy with their leadership role when mapping took hold in their building. They worked hard with their teachers during the year and their instructional leadership is now clearly defined in their mapping work.

Leadership at all levels, both formal and informal, is critical to sustain the mapping process in any district. As the curriculum mapping work in the district has changed from data entry to dialogue about the maps, the building administrators began to assume a greater role. Monthly administrative meetings have been focused on discussions about the building administrators' leadership role with mapping. As their understanding of mapping has grown, they are now doing an excellent job in leading this work in their buildings.

There were several things that took place at our administrative meetings that helped to build more leaders and increase proficiency with the mapping process. A good deal of our time at administrative evening meetings was spent discussing recently published curriculum mapping books. We also spent time sharing tips and new learning regarding the software. The time spent on these topics helped to increase the comfort and leadership roles among our administrators.

Upon reflection, there are several things we would do differently in regard to developing shared leadership earlier in the process:

- Begin with both formal and informal leaders at all levels— teacher leaders and administrators—well in advance of mapping.
- Clearly articulate the goals of the process and build in benchmark assessments to assess the goals.
- Identify the roles each party will play and the expectations of those roles.

Table 5.2   Action Plan, Year Two

Year	Key Action	Person Responsible/Involved
Year Two 2005–2006	Establish District Curriculum Mapping Cabinet	Representatives from each building (Elementary – 1 each, Secondary – 2 each = Total of 15 to 20 members) Building principals to form council, see attached for list of required members West Middle – all teachers
	Establish building-level Curriculum Mapping Councils	East Middle – selected departments West Senior – design team headed by department chair East Senior – design team headed by department chair
	Start mapping with design teams at middle and high schools	Trained by: Tribuzzi, Wiley, Beehler, Todorof, secondary principals Secondary teachers new to mapping – AM session Elementary teachers with mapping experience – PM session
	Tri-annual CM Cabinet meetings	Building Council (see attached for breakdown of each council at the various levels) Building principals and teacher leaders facilitate meetings, faculty discussions Building principals, directors, and department chairs facilitate meetings, faculty discussions
	Building Council meets periodically; plan/coordinate mapping efforts in the building	
	Read-through of maps, review of curriculum maps (elementary level)	
	Continue mapping at secondary level – use maps in faculty, team and department meetings	

- Continually revisit and communicate the vision.
- Write out the vision statement and the action plan for all to read.
- Share the plan with district technicians and confer more closely to be sure that the hardware and operating systems in each building are compatible with mapping software and able to handle the Internet traffic.
- Further promote open and honest dialogue among administrators and teachers, allowing for discourse about differing opinions and interests.

In hindsight, the establishment of the leadership team, and the development of a common vision and clear action plan should have been more solidly established before we asked teachers to begin to map. A clear vision and confidence in the leaders' mapping skills needed to support the process would have avoided some of the growing pains we've experienced.

ZOOMING IN ON TWO SCHOOLS

The engine of improvement, growth, and renewal in a PLC is collective inquiry. People in such a community are relentless in questioning the status quo, seeking new methods, testing those methods, and then reflecting on the results. Not only do they have an acute sense of curiosity and openness to new possibilities, they also recognize that the process of searching for answers is more important than having an answer.

—DuFour, 1998

Professional Learning Communities

One of the goals of mapping is the development of a professional learning community. For this goal to be accomplished, it must start at the leadership level, but involve all those that are expected to share and support the vision. In our elementary buildings, this feeling of trust and sharing has taken hold through mapping. Mrs. Tana Cleveland, principal of Potters Road Elementary School, exhibits an example of strong building leadership. She explains her efforts with mapping below.

In many ways our building was ready for curriculum mapping. Grade-level teachers had a daily, common planning time in place. Though some instructional discussion occurred, this time was mainly utilized for individual planning, duplication, recordkeeping, and the never-ending parent communication. Thus common planning time did little to support professional learning communities. To encourage quality grade-level conversations, the monthly, large group, principal-directed faculty meetings were replaced by small grade-level meetings, which were held in classrooms. Grade-levels discussed pacing, planning, and preparation. Brief, sentence fragment minutes kept me informed of the meeting focus. Though I attended meetings when invited, professional conversations were happening, to my delight, without me. Quarterly, in-school meetings between the reading personnel, the literacy teacher, the enrichment teacher, and all members of the grade level provided an opportunity to discuss strategies, materials, and pacing. When I attended my first curriculum mapping session, I knew mapping could weave together our conversations on content, skills, assessment, and materials.

The planning for our journey into curriculum mapping began well before September 2005, when mapping would become the vehicle by which we all communicated our instruction. If mapping was to be successful it could not be an additional task, it had to be the core. To try to make this happen, efforts were made to have routine requirements, such as the yearly Building Professional Development Plan and the Professional Study Plan, focus on mapping or include a mapping strand. Everything had to tie together. When we were asked to submit names of teachers to serve on the design team, I carefully considered and selected a cross-grade-level group of teachers who were respected by their colleagues and who clearly shared the vision of why we needed to be mapping. Teachers were invited to participate in early mapping information sessions with my acknowledgment that they were building leaders and master teachers.

When mapping days were scheduled, I attended with teachers and went from grade-level group to grade-level group listening for concerns. Our building team would later meet to determine what needed to happen in our building to support mapping. Attending work sessions with teachers is imperative. Your attendance as the building principal proves your commitment to them. The trouble-shooting we did together during the first year helped to lessen obstacles that could impede the successful formation of the learning communities necessary for our mapping work to evolve.

In the second year of mapping, as our "Building Curriculum Council" was formed, five to six new individuals were asked to participate and join the design team with the common goal of supporting mapping in the building. Because of this safe and inviting atmosphere we attempted to create, some common concerns among the teachers rose to the surface and we have tried to address them along the way.

Time was a huge concern to teachers. They barely had time to complete their plan books, locate materials, call parents, and yes, instruct, without the added stress of mapping each month after they had already accomplished the instruction. To lessen this concern, all administrators in the district agreed to waive the completion and submission of plan books for those who were mapping. We put this in writing and only required plan books from new teachers. Personally, even though I knew this was the right move to support teachers and mapping, this was tough for me. Plan books had long been the way for me to keep my finger on the pulse of the classrooms. Now I felt as though I didn't have a clue as to what was happening in the building. Here, my faith in the teachers kicked in. I was able to take the leap of faith because I firmly believed that all teachers were doing their best whether or not they were documenting it in tiny plan book boxes. To regain the feeling that I knew what was going on in the building, I facilitated monthly mapping sessions. With the technology now available, it is very easy for anyone to access the maps and get valuable information about their instruction.

Removing the plan book requirement was a start, but time to map was still needed. Again, the district came to the rescue by providing substitutes to allow teachers to physically map their diary maps. A monthly schedule was developed that provided either two-hour or half-day mapping sessions so that each teacher had the opportunity to map with moral and technical support at least once a month. I attended every mapping session as a beginner. It was quickly established that I was learning right along with the mappers. We have been fortunate enough to have a consultant from the local Board of Cooperative Educational Services (BOCES) support us frequently enough to help teachers and me with our technical questions and our growing expertise. I keep a journal of each mapping session. I noted who was in the group and their concerns, successes, and needs. I took note of those who needed more technical support than I was capable of providing and where we needed to go to have questions answered for the next month. In a few cases, tutorials were arranged. Today one of the most technologically challenged teachers is answering questions for the group!

The technology was new and so was the mapping process. Many mappers were challenged by both factors. Proficiency with the technology came quite quickly. Like any student, teachers were fearful that their maps weren't perfect. If the maps looked complete, they also wanted feedback to tell them that. Each mapping session would start with a brief mini-lesson on mapping basics such as what a diary map is, or how content statements are clearly communicated. At this point we couldn't answer the question, "What does a perfect map look like?" so we focused on some "Quality Indicators" based on mapping details that were observable.

We felt that we needed to build teacher confidence with the mapping process. We knew that if we outlined some simple, achievable benchmarks by which their maps would be judged by their team, it would increase teacher confidence. This turned out to be a good step in bringing down the anxiety level of all involved.

Once the "language" of a quality map was defined, we began to focus on the alignment process and how that process tied the items together in a quality map. The direction was to align through content in order to show how all of the pieces of the map went together.

The process and time that was involved in defining the quality mapping indicators was worth the effort as the faculty began to feel more at ease with the way they were articulating their maps.

Mappers needed to feel proficient and the design of these quality indicators gave us a clear place to start. As maps are turned in monthly, I make certain to comment on the quality indicators that are in place before returning the maps. As we grow together, the depth of these indicators has also grown. One month my secretary accidentally returned maps before I had commented on them. Immediately teachers were coming to me asking if anything was wrong with their maps because there were no comments. Taking the time to provide specific feedback on maps is important and appreciated by beginning mappers.

With each month we develop growing competency with mapping and an understanding of the language. Mappers have the tendency to want to back up and change previous months. We have agreed that once you are done with a particular month you should not go back and revise until the following year. New knowledge should be applied to future maps.

Our building committee heard and communicated the need for our mapping vision to be reinforced and communicated frequently. The first few months of mapping were difficult and often teachers began asking, "Why are we doing this again?" I believe that as the months passed and important instructional conversations emerged, the need to continually repeat the vision lessened. Conversations during the mapping became rich and focused on student achievement, assessment, gaps, alignment, resources, and strategies. As the depth of conversation increased, the vision was automatically reinforced on a personal level. To me, these conversations are the most exciting part of the mapping process and I am quick to comment on these exchanges. Providing a non-judgmental and opening line of communication is important to build trust and a willingness to share amongst your teaching staff. The vision must be honestly embraced by the building leader. Teachers know when you believe in something. Your commitment cannot be fractional or occasional.

ADDRESSING OBSTACLES THAT CAN IMPEDE PROGRESS

Time

Perhaps the biggest obstacle many districts and schools face when beginning curriculum mapping is that dirty, four-letter word—TIME! Educators are constantly pressed to complete more duties and demands in less time. In fact, of all the industrialized nations in the world, the United States has the shortest school day and year of them all. William Bainbridge tells us, "American students have a shorter school year than those living in 12 of the world's other wealthiest nations. Students in other information-age countries receive twice as much instruction as American students in core academic areas during their secondary school years."

Mapping is initially a time-intensive process that requires teachers to think purposefully about their instruction, while trying to articulate it in a way that everyone can understand. Time is needed for a variety of tasks:

- Communicating the vision to your staff.
- Training your faculty/staff on data entry: The first year of mapping is the most time intensive because you are creating maps from scratch (either diary or essential maps). Data entry is further complicated when technology gets in the way or impedes teachers who are less savvy with technology.
- Reading the maps: Time must be spent early in the process to review maps and determine if we are creating quality maps that everyone can read and understand. Our mantra has become, "Don't map crap!"
- Curriculum dialogues: Further time is needed for teachers to meet collaboratively to review the maps and discuss instruction, curriculum, and assessment.

Of all the processes that require time, especially in the first year of mapping, the one that our teachers have needed the most guidance with was data entry. There was often anxiety and apprehension, as they hoped and wondered if they were "doing it right." Mapping is not a means to an end—the process will evolve and change—but it will never be finished. As educators, we are often compelled to finish a task cleanly and move on to the next. The process of mapping is a paradigm shift for many. After the initial year of data entry, all mapping software will archive teachers' units that they have created. In subsequent years, they will be returning to those units to modify and tweak them based on their instruction for that year and those students. The units themselves may or may not change. In the evolution of this process, the data input work should lessen and the dialogues become more prominent—thus, working smarter and not harder.

To assist teachers in fighting the time battle, we offer several solutions that may fit your reality. This list is not exhaustive or perfect, but offers some suggestions that we are using to help move the process along.

Common planning time for grade levels or departments

Often when crafting schedules, building principals can carve out time for like-minded groups to meet, either as a grade level or department. Even if provided once or twice a week, it would build in a common time for these individuals to meet and discuss their curriculum maps.

Table 5.3   Action Plan, Year Three

Obstacle	Descriptions of the Obstacle	Potential Solutions
Leadership	Leadership at all levels, both formal and informal, are critical. A "shared leadership" approach that involves teachers and administrators is critical. Uninvolved or uninformed leaders can certainly block the progress of the well-intended teachers. We have seen districts send teachers to an initial training with no administrative support or presence. It takes both groups to make it succeed.	• Involve both formal and informal leaders from all levels—teachers and administration • Clearly articulate the goals of the process and build in benchmarks to assess the plan • Identify the roles all parties will play • Continually revisit and communicate the vision • Develop common expectations and requirements across the district
Time	Time will be needed for a variety of tasks: communicating the vision, training, data entry, and collaboration/discussion about the maps. Teachers and administrators find the time they have to map and meet about their maps very limited. A limited amount of professional development time may be available or provided for mapping.	• Common plan/mapping time for grade levels or departments • Release time with substitute coverage • Summer curriculum mapping time • Professional development courses after or before school • Faculty/department meetings • Superintendent's conference days • Action research • Discontinue practices that could save time (i.e., formal lesson plans)
Training	Teachers will need a variety of training opportunities focused on curriculum mapping and how to utilize the technology to complete the maps. The "skill" of mapping takes time to develop and refine. Early conversation will focus on the mechanics of creating quality maps. Subsequent meetings will move to the content of the maps.	• Provide consistent training to all faculty/staff • Use time available—conference days or release time • Consult with trainers from a software company or private consultant • Develop district norms to establish a consistent model of what a quality map is
Personalities	Resistant teachers will exist in every environment. Teachers that resist the process or do not understand the purpose of mapping.	• Empty chair concept • Utilize curriculum cabinet/councils • Provide opportunities for input • Mentors/coaches to work with teachers
Resources	Some districts cannot afford to utilize online software or products. Sometimes providing time to map or release time for teachers is cost-prohibitive.	• Use grant and title monies • Work with local agencies or other districts to pool resources • Value the people who add to the effort!

Release time with coverage, "Curriculum Dialogue Meetings"

This would be time provided to teachers during their workday to enter data and discuss their maps, usually by providing a substitute teacher. In our district, we provide each elementary principal two days a month where they get eight substitutes for the day. They can utilize them however they desire, covering teachers for two hours, half of the day, or an entire day. This allows them the flexibility to create mixed groups for review or additional time for teachers to complete diary maps. In one of our schools, teachers take turns supervising and dismissing students at the end of the day to create a 30-minute window for their colleagues to work on their maps.

Summer curriculum mapping time

Many school districts earmark money for curriculum writing or development. The summer offers a less stressful and relaxed time to bring in groups of teachers to work on curriculum maps or develop their mapping skills.

Faculty/department meetings

Faculty meetings in many schools still tend to be used as an information sharing or "administrivia" period. Items that could easily be disseminated through an email to faculty members litter long agendas. Instead, these periods of time could be used for powerful curriculum sharing and dialogue amongst faculty.

Superintendent's conference days

Districts that formally build professional development days into their school year need to use this time wisely. It is easy to schedule the "sit and get" professional development day where several hundred teachers are herded into an auditorium to be enlightened by a world-renowned keynote speaker. This is the playground for teachers who need to catch-up on their crossword puzzle, knitting, or magazine reading. While we have all used this format and it sometimes serves a purpose, we need to think differently about how to use these precious days.

Professional development after hours

It became increasingly obvious to us that there simply is not enough time during the school day to accomplish everything we need to do, nor can we always wait for the summer. The West Seneca Teachers' Center is located within our district and provides professional development opportunities on a variety of topics. To be responsive to the needs of our teachers, they agreed to develop a series of workshops for the teachers to help them further develop their proficiency with mapping. Each course is three hours in length, with about an hour of focused instruction, and approximately two hours of mapping and sharing time. One course, for example, is about using the reports that can be generated by the software. In this class, participants spend time exploring the various reports available to them in the software and then discuss when each would be useful to use. These targeted courses focus on different aspects of mapping that all of our teachers need to develop over time. These specific and targeted courses provide differentiated training, while allowing them to complete the data entry process.

Action research

Every district has a process for evaluating the performance of their teachers. Our teachers follow a three-year review cycle. In year one, an administrator, using the Framework for Teaching Model developed by Charlotte Danielson (1996), formally observes them. In their second or third year, they are required to complete a Professional Study Plan (PSP) in which they research a topic and implement change in their instruction as a result. For example, a high school social studies teacher may desire to learn more about teaching literacy skills through the content. She would spend two years researching best practice strategies in how to teach reading and writing in the content area and implement some of those strategies.

Increasingly, we are encouraging teachers to build in curriculum mapping as part of the evidence collection process. Several groups of teachers have also opted to conduct book studies focusing on curriculum mapping as part of their study plan. There is one word of caution that is critical here. Our district does not and will not utilize curriculum maps to evaluate teachers! It is important to not use them punitively or to criticize teachers or the essence of a professional learning community will be lost. Not to mention, if I know that you will use these maps to evaluate my performance, I may be more inclined to populate my map with what I think you want to see instead of what I actually did with my students.

Discontinue unneeded practices

Teachers and administrators often feel as if their plate is overflowing. Unfortunately, some districts just advocate getting a bigger plate instead of deciding what can come off the plate!

Training to Develop Necessary Skills

Training and time go hand in hand. The software we chose showed great promise to enhance communication and viability for the curriculum, but was also especially exciting because of the various reports and data it could provide for teachers to review. Once we made a decision about which curriculum mapping tool we would use, we began to plan the training for teachers with this tool. In many ways, using a technology application for mapping has made all the difference. At any time, teachers can search and analyze maps created by another teacher anywhere in the district or even the world. The concept of a professional learning community can now stretch far outside the walls of West Seneca to a global community. The information entered into maps can be formulated in reports to allow teachers to review, critique, and analyze their instruction. One report that is commonly used is "Standards Addressed in Maps," in which teachers can find out how many times they have taught to certain performance indicators. This could not have been done easily or effectively using lessons in plan books.

Despite the major advantages that technology has provided, one must remember that not all teachers are ready for what they may perceive as "technology overload." In our thinking, there are basically four different types of mappers you will quickly identify in training sessions:

- "I don't get it!" Mapper: These are individuals who do not have a clear understanding of why we are mapping. In addition to this, they are not usually proficient in the use of the technology.
- "Show me to the computer!" Mapper: These teachers are quite good at using the computer and understand the software. However, they may have trouble grasping the mapping concepts and how to create a quality map.
- "Can I do this on paper?" Mapper: This individual is quite good at grasping why mapping is taking place and can articulate their instruction, but they are not comfortable with the software or feel as if the technology just slows them down.
- "Big picture" Mapper: This person is a trainer's delight. They understand why we are mapping, what the characteristics of a quality map look like, and how to enter them into the software efficiently.

The challenge will be to identify where all of your teachers fall on this continuum and provide support for all. In the beginning, we had (and still have) teachers who were the "I don't get it" variety. Increasingly, we must hope to move more of our teachers through sustained staff development and support to the "big picture" phase.

Technology

One of our stumbling blocks with the training early on was the actual technology in the district. West Seneca is extremely fortunate to have a robust technology infrastructure. However, as a Mac-based district, we had several different operating systems on the computers in different buildings. We also worked with teachers who were more proficient on PCs than on Macs. The mapping software company worked hard to answer our questions and facilitate the process, but eventually we were responsible for maintaining an accurate database of teachers and making account changes. Be sure to include your technology leaders in the implementation process from the start.

As the number of mapping teachers increased, the need for support grew as well. It was no longer possible for two trainers to sustain the ongoing needs of teachers as they began to engage themselves in mapping. In addition to frequent coaching over the phone from our mapping consultants, we consulted with some leaders in the field. As we experienced early uncertainty and had questions about how to sustain success, we invited these leaders to address our teaching and administrative staff. This professional development involved a keynote address from Dr. Heidi Hayes Jacobs. A national consultant, Janet Hale, also helped educate us on different levels of maps and the formulation of mapping "norms." Lastly, we have also utilized the services of an educational local service center, Board of Cooperative Educational Services (BOCES), to help provide training and support. Utilizing this service also helped make some of the costs associated with mapping reimbursable. Be sure to investigate what products or services are available through your local educational service provider if that structure exists.

Personalities

Change in a district tends to bring out the best in some people, and fear or resistance in others. Michael Fullan (1994) wrote, "Change can be likened to a planned journey into uncharted waters in a leaky boat with a mutinous crew." It is important to minimize the number of individuals who feel the need to be "mutinous." Several of our missteps have allowed us to better understand how to accomplish this feat. First, it is critical to involve teacher leaders in the process from the beginning. The teachers' union should also be kept in the loop of the action plan so that as changes in district operations take place, they won't appear haphazard to anyone involved.

When studying what will be required to undertake mapping successfully, identify key teacher leaders and involve them in the discussion. Secondly, create structures that allow for a clear flow of communication and feedback. Reflection tells us that more attention to these elements may have helped to make the vision clearer.

If you work in a district that has a history of initiatives coming and going, teachers will naturally be reluctant to "buy-in" to what they perceive to be the latest fad. Why did these previous efforts fail? The answers could include a number of reasons, including a change in leadership, a poorly crafted and communicated plan, or perhaps diminished resources.

This opens the door for the familiar refrain, "Didn't we already do this?" or "We tried this before and it didn't work!" In addition, every school will have a portion of their faculty that is reluctant to change for one reason or another. How then, do we engage these individuals so that we can build a critical mass within our schools?

Empty Chair Concept

When Heidi Hayes Jacobs presents to groups, she begins by placing an empty chair in the front of the room. She then solicits the name of a student from a teacher in the group. We'll call the student Chris. Chris represents all of our students, and each teacher can usually identify "Chris" in their own classroom. The concept that she advocates is that all discussion and decisions must be focused on what is in Chris' best interest.

Occasionally, we will meet with teachers who want to question or criticize the process of mapping. First, we allow it. It is only through discourse and discussion that some issues can be solved. Yet, if the conversation leads to solutions or excuses that are not in Chris' best interest, the conversation is redirected. Unfortunately, some educators do not always make decisions based on what is in the best interest of the student. Secondly, once an issue or problem is raised, we must also provide equal time to discuss potential solutions. In a true professional learning community, teachers and administrators must be free to express concerns and ideas without fear of ridicule or punitive measures. However, if a person expresses criticism of the process, we've asked them to be willing to provide some potential solutions to make it work. There is a saying we have used to illustrate this point: "If you are not part of the solution, you must be part of the problem."

SHARED INPUT AND DECISION MAKING

Districts that create oversight or steering committees to plan and navigate the mapping process allow for teacher input. Our process began as a "top-down" initiative and we lacked significant input from teachers and administrators. As more of the obstacles surfaced, it became clear that we needed a more formal forum for input and problem solving.

Curriculum Cabinet/Councils

One thing we attempted to do early on in the process was assemble a District Curriculum Cabinet. Because school districts rarely complete existing initiatives before they begin another, we had to bring a few district-level groups to closure before we could introduce another. Although we would have preferred to have this group in place earlier, the delayed start allowed us to choose members who would help to move the process forward. This group was formed in our second year and was charged with the responsibility of clarifying the vision and goals for mapping, monitoring, and making recommendations about the action plan, and deciding how future training will take place. This group will also serves as the main vehicle by which to communicate these decisions. These teachers and administrators will look at the overarching needs, gaps, and redundancies in the curriculum and will work as task forces to solve issues relating to mapping.

In addition, each building has created a site-based curriculum leadership council. This council is empowered to assist the building administrator in carrying out the mapping process in each building. They help plan staff development, train and coach the teachers, review the maps, and make decisions about curriculum and instruction at the building level. Our hope is that one or more members of the building council will also sit on the district-level group. They will serve as the link between what is decided at both levels and communicate these decisions to everyone involved.

Regardless of what structures are put in place or what you actually call these groups, the groups must include teachers and administrators! This provides the opportunity for all constituents to have a voice in how the curriculum mapping process unfolds and builds within a district or school. It specifically gets at several of the goals previously stated in the chapter—it serves as a forum for communication, collaboration, and coaching. Make no mistake about it. This body of individuals should have clearly identified jobs. Members can be grouped into specific task forces that work on issues that arise. In our case, we have a professional development task force, a mapping technology task force, and other task forces that will target specific areas of need. The discussions and recommendations from these groups will provide a voice that represents all stakeholders in the district.

So what role does the resistant teacher play in these committees? Typically, it seems that the same teachers serve on all the committees we have. In fact, if you are an eager and cooperative teacher, you are likely "rewarded" by serving on many different teams in your school. We'd argue that you must also invite some of the naysayers to the party. They represent an important, often vocal group. Their opinions and even criticisms are important to address during the process. What may appear to be teacher resistance during the change process must be considered carefully. Teacher resistance can instead be seen as a necessary component that will eventually emit suggestions that will help make the work make sense to everyone. Passionate teachers can move an organization toward resiliency and self-renewal because their input can help the work evolve into successful practice.

DuFour (1998) explains in his work that collaborative teams are a central piece to developing professional learning communities. He writes:

> The basic structure of the professional learning community is a group of collaborative teams that share a common purpose. Some organizations base their improvement strategies on efforts to enhance the knowledge and skills of individuals. Although individual growth is essential for organizational growth to occur, it does not *guarantee* organizational growth. Thus, building a school's capacity to learn is a collaborative rather than an individual task. People who engage in collaborative team learning are able to learn from one another, thus creating momentum to fuel improvement.

RESOURCES AND INCENTIVES

There were several decisions made at the district level early on in the process to help provide the resources to support the process of mapping. The West Seneca District believes in providing professional development to build capacity in the teaching staff. We have typically received support from the school board, superintendent, and assistant superintendent for curriculum and instruction to provide teachers with opportunities to attend conferences to increase their knowledge. Although these opportunities have been an important element in the district, it was agreed to suspend most of the conferences that teachers would attend for the first years of mapping in order to redirect the funds to pay for substitutes to provide coverage during mapping sessions.

The district budget includes funds for curriculum writing efforts that often take place each summer. Examining those processes and making changes that now require teachers to use the mapping program as the vehicle by which they create projection maps has replaced the previous practice of "writing" new curriculum. This has allowed directors of the content areas to contract teachers to help with the mapping initiative and compensate them for their time in the summer or after school.

The other resources that cannot go unmentioned are the efforts of the administrators and teachers who have helped to lead this initiative in the district. It is the time and effort that committed teachers and administrators have put into the process to make it work to this point. Jean Kovach, the assistant superintendent for curriculum and instruction, was instrumental in supporting the mapping initiative and providing constant support and resources. Without her brainstorming sessions and encouragement to work toward an aligned curriculum, the progress we've made in two years would not have been possible. Committed and hard working people are probably the most valuable resource a district can have. It is the people, after all, that will make the change process possible.

Examining Data and Curriculum Maps

Using data to make decisions in schools is essential in today's era of accountability. We can no longer make decisions based on our hunches, and curriculum mapping helps to bridge the gap between what is taught and the results of those efforts. Although we've had assessment data to analyze in the past, we can now look at the combination of the operational curriculum and the related assessment data. This is a powerful combination with which educators can make decisions to improve achievement. It will take time to have maps that are complete enough to reflect what really happens in an elementary classroom, but once the data is in the maps, it can be analyzed against assessment data.

Brian Graham, principal of Winchester Elementary School, has worked diligently to help his teachers move beyond simply creating their diary maps. In his curriculum dialogue meetings, he is able to utilize mapping and assessment data to focus the discussions with his teachers.

> *The information we collect and analyze should help us understand and improve instructional processes that help get better results.*
>
> —Schmoker, 1996

Graham leads his entire faculty through the beginning of the mapping initiative. His reflections follow:

Each Halloween season, the faculty and staff at Winchester Elementary School gather for a festive costume breakfast. This year, I decided to attend as "Data-Man," that new educational superhero you may have seen who assimilates and disaggregates test score results faster than a speeding bullet. All of the teachers who attended the breakfast that day definitely saw the humor in my choice of costume. Data is a word that I use quite a bit because I rely on data to inform many decisions related to the instructional practices at Winchester. With guidance and a continued focus on data analysis and use, Winchester teachers have become quite proficient at using data to inform their daily classroom practice.

Before the 2005–2006 school year, data analysis related to the New York State English Language Arts Assessment. A team consisting of teachers for Grades 3 and 4, along with members of our reading department, our special education teachers, and our enrichment teacher met regularly in order to analyze assessment data focusing both on student achievement and test construct. We would deconstruct the previous assessment and analyze the embedded literacy skills while also paying close attention to the NYS standards and performance indicators. In the early days of our work as a team, all of the analysis was completed painstakingly by hand and later transferred into an "AppleWorks" spreadsheet. It was quickly evident that we needed a more efficient way to gather, examine, and analyze the results of our fourth graders. Each year that the team engaged in this type of analysis, we craved information that would be more meaningful. We needed the data to provide the answers to some questions that would help us effectively inform instructional practice. We wanted to use our results from previous years to examine for trends that may have existed positively or negatively. We wanted to see if there were any trends in our looping patterns, or specific classrooms. We wanted to see if there were any trends related to specific literacy skill development or trends in the acquisition of NYS performance indicators that may have been assessed frequently over the past three years.

With the help of our district's Chief Information Officer and some self-taught skills in Microsoft Excel, we quickly began working smarter by decreasing the time it took to input the data. This process allowed us to focus on the analysis and the action plans that could be created based upon the information. Once the action plan was created, Winchester teachers implemented the plan and then we held our collective breath as a new batch of fourth graders were assessed by New York State. We met as a vertical group with the third and fourth grade teachers who worked with the same group of students for two years as part of our looping initiative. The worst component of this whole process was the "collective holding our breath" part. Although we had spent the time analyzing the data from our fourth graders each year and creating action plans, we had to wait several months for the ELA results to come back to us from NYS before the team could measure the success of our hard work. This system of testing is flawed because it involves a large gap of time before the results are shared and changes in the design and implementation of the curriculum can be created. What the team really needed was student information collected over time that paralleled the NYS assessment. The data needed to be formative in nature. We needed to combine that data with a mechanism for tracking the operational curriculum that reflects the actual instruction and assessment that takes place in the classroom on a daily basis rather than a projection of what should be taught.

> *Schmoker (1996) points out that the foundation for showing positive results in student achievement comes from meaningful teamwork combined with setting clear goals and regularly collecting and analyzing performance data.*

Winchester served as a pilot school for the curriculum mapping initiative in the district. The initiative started with an emphasis on diary mapping the English and Language Arts operational curriculum that is lived and breathed in each classroom. In conjunction with the mapping, the district implemented the Comprehensive Assessment of Reading Strategies (CARS) in Grades 2–8. The CARS assessments are designed to identify students' weaknesses and strengths in twelve standards-based reading strategies from Grades 2–6. The twelve strategies assessed are:

- Finding Main Idea
- Recalling Facts and Details
- Understanding Sequence
- Recognizing Cause and Effect
- Comparing and Contrasting
- Making Predictions
- Finding Word Meaning in Context
- Drawing Conclusions and Making Inferences
- Distinguishing Between Fact and Opinion
- Identifying Author's Purpose
- Interpreting Figurative Language
- Summarizing

In order to use the data generated from CARS in a timely and efficient manner, our literacy specialist collects the achievement data relating to the CARS assessments every six to seven weeks. The data are organized in a master spreadsheet. The spreadsheet allows us to sort the information by student, teacher, grade, or skill. The team can now generate reports every two months to specifically identify which strategies our students are proficient and which strategies need more attention. The data are used to provide guidance for student placement into our academic intervention services program. Data-based academic intervention leads to the employment of targeted, differentiated instructional practices that benefit our students, as well as providing information to assess growth and progress toward identified standards, strategies, and skills.

With the diary mapping initiative in full swing and a systematic plan in place to assess specific higher order thinking skills on a regular basis, the team had the opportunity to use mapping to uncover the use of these skills across all curricular areas and across all grade levels. In the monthly curriculum mapping meetings, grade-level teams used the Curriculum Analyzer tool in the TechPaths mapping software program to generate data related to the twelve strategies assessed in CARS. Curriculum Analyzer allows a search through all diary maps in a building or specific grade level. The search can be done by keyword and quickly yields information regarding how often a strategy is addressed in the diary maps. The keyword related to the strategy, such as figurative language, is entered into Curriculum Analyzer and the search is conducted by user choice in one of the following areas:

- Essential Questions
- Content
- Skills
- Assessments
- Lessons
- Standards

The Curriculum Analyzer prompts the user to identify the department where the search should be conducted, such as Art, Music, Physical Education, Reading, English, Math, or Science. The grade level and building can be searched as well. When TechPaths displays the results of the search, a Web-based report is generated. This report is organized by teacher, grade range, month, and total. What you see is a listing of teachers in your building that have documented teaching the skill of figurative language. You will see how often a teacher has documented the skill of figurative language as content within a diary map. You will notice that the same piece of content is also identified as a skill that was taught to the students. You will also see how many times that skill was assessed during that particular month. Each number is hyperlinked back to the author's diary map. The power of this one report lies in the ability to tailor the conversations around mapping in order to focus on specific building initiatives that are designed to enhance student achievement related to identified gaps in the instruction and assessment of target strategies. Teachers can generate this report at any time so that data analysis can occur at times other than scheduled grade-level curriculum mapping conversation. The report is hyperlinked so that the teacher can get new ideas on how to address a specific ELA skill or strategy from their colleagues who have maps in TechPaths.

Dawn Voelker, a looping teacher from first grade, indicates: "Since diary mapping, I have found that I am more aware of the skills that I am teaching. Although very time consuming, it helps me plan accordingly and allows me to see what I am over-teaching or under-teaching. Furthermore, it gives me the opportunity to focus on the needs of my children and address them accordingly. I like the ability to see other teachers' maps. When I am looking for a new way to address content, I just search the maps and see what comes up. Once I find something I like, I can copy it (and send them a thank you) or make it my own. This is like a little "light bulb moment." Then I say to myself, "Hey, why didn't I think of that?" It really allows me to see how others are thinking."

Barb DuCotey, a kindergarten teacher, states: "As I curriculum map, I notice the skills that I have not spent enough time on. I think about the class as a whole, and then I think about individuals, and add these skills to my next week's (month's) plans. I may work on these skills in a large group setting, if most of the class needs it, or I may work on them in small groups for the few children who need the extra help on a skill. I also notice if I have spent too much time on various skills."

The district provides data regarding three-year achievement trends on the NYS ELA assessments. That type of data helps define achievement trends at Winchester. For example, fourth graders have performed poorly when asked questions on the NYS ELA Grade 4 assessments in the area of using graphic organizers for information and understanding. In fact, Winchester has performed the lowest in the district when compared with six other elementary buildings. The data provide a performance indicator comparison for the entire region as well. This particular skill has been assessed using seven different questions on the past three NYS ELA Grade 4 assessments. When this trend was identified during curriculum mapping grade-level meetings, the teachers all took note of the trend and began to consider creative ways to increase the use of graphic organizers for information and understanding, and how to document the increased emphasis on this strategy within their diary maps. From this point forward, the information gathered from the use of the Curriculum Analyzer can provide an analysis focus and the impact of our targeted initiatives can be measured. Since our focus on the use of graphic organizers began, evidence from the diary maps has indicated an increased use and assessment of the strategy. To take this analysis to a deeper level, the teachers can bring samples of student work to the curriculum mapping grade-level meetings in order to share ideas related to instruction. The quantitative data derived from the maps is supplemented by the qualitative data found in the student samples in order to create a multi-dimensional implementation of the targeted strategy.

Through the curriculum mapping process, teachers are able to document the operational curriculum in their classroom as well as provide evidence of the differentiated instructional strategies designed to address the targeted skills and strategies. These curriculum mapping conversations provide a vehicle by which to address the building-wide goal of integrating ELA across the content areas. Teachers in all subject areas can participate in the discussions and have access to the data in order to consider how the targeted strategy applies in their classrooms. Certainly, the expectation is that teachers in all areas, from art to physical education to social studies, can use the targeted skills and strategies within the context of their specific curriculum. When this cross-curricular implementation happens, all students will have access to this particular skill living and breathing within the operational curriculum in all of their classes. When the mapping process is focused on specific goals, teachers see how the integration of content, skills, and assessments with specific achievement data directly influences student success.

Jennifer Szewc, a second grade teacher, states, "In the past, I taught the book *Frog and Toad are Friends* by Arnold Lobel. We would read each chapter, focus on new vocabulary, and answer some comprehension questions. After seeing the fall CARS test results and looking at the areas of deficiency my students had, I decided to pull apart the book and address the skills that the second-graders had scored below 50%. For example, "figurative language" was a skill that I had only addressed twice on my September curriculum map and the children scored 25% proficiency on that strategy in October. So, I created a brand new curriculum for the story. I have also made sure that I address that skill through at least one story during each month. The students have improved in that strategy since October and in February 64% of the students in my class have a better understanding of figurative language. I know exactly where it has been addressed because it is on my curriculum map."

Payne (2003) suggests that when schools begin to function at an epistemic level, data is integrated at all levels allowing teachers to help students to function at the meta-cognitive level.

State assessments ask students to perform at the meta-cognitive level. To get students to work at the meta-cognitive level, the system must function at the epistemic level. In other words, districts must have an integrated, systems approach for everything. A district cannot lead if it is at the same level as its students. Many systems right now are fragmented and operate at the mind level. They can talk about the system but cannot represent it in any kind of an abstract representational manner. The data are largely anecdotal. When a system operates at the meta-cognitive level, officials can give you the computer printouts, the graphs, and the charts. But the data are not integrated. When a district is operating at the epistemic level, data are integrated. All programs are integrated. Professional dialogue is structured (Payne, 2003).

Winchester literacy specialist Kim McCartan says, "It is easy to see how we need to focus on the standards and performance indicators for ELA. For the first time, as a teacher, a grade level, a building, a district, etc., we are able to analyze what we are doing. I guess what I am trying to ask is—we may talk the talk, but are we actually walking the walk? We may put it in our plans, and maps, but is that matching up to what we are doing in our classrooms? Does it match the way our students are performing? We may drive by those standards, but are we actually looking at them and using them. Diary mapping allows us to compare our assessments to what is happening in the classroom on a daily basis."

By making full use of our curriculum mapping software and by effectively integrating mapping with data analysis, Winchester is moving toward an epistemic operational model that focuses on student achievement. Even though the "Data-Man" costume is gathering dust in a closet, the faculty, administration, and staff of Winchester proudly wear the mantle of data team in their work each day.

SUMMARY

The West Seneca School District is now moving in a direction that promises to reveal new possibilities with curriculum development and analysis. It has not been an easy process, and the work will never end. The work, however, is changing. We are finally moving from data input to curriculum dialogue and the level of conversation about teaching and learning at the teacher and administrative levels are unprecedented. The curriculum focus and expectations in the district are at a higher level than ever before. This hard work has already begun to provide dividends in that we're examining our practices and identifying issues that require additional professional development or further investigation.

Our journey through curriculum mapping is most certainly a good example of what DuFour (1998) refers to as *collective inquiry*.

The engine of improvement, growth, and renewal in a Professional Learning Community (PLC) is collective inquiry. People in such a community are relentless in questioning the status quo, seeking new methods, testing those methods, and then reflecting on the results. Not only do they have an acute sense of curiosity and openness to new possibilities, they also recognize that the process of searching for answers is more important than having an answer.

What is difficult in this journey is moving away from the status quo and realizing the value in the **process versus the product**. Indeed, we are confident that our efforts will be realized through alignment between curriculum, instruction, and assessment. Yet, those of you who will work tirelessly listening, prompting, massaging, and coaching your teachers through this process will undoubtedly see the value in the discussion that comes about as a *result* of curriculum mapping. In the process, school leaders and teachers continually need to develop new skills to support the changing work that technology lends itself to. We must remember to celebrate our growth and successes in order to energize and affirm the hard work that lies ahead. We will celebrate our progress as we move closer to reaching our goals toward increased rigor through an aligned K–12 curriculum.

6 Case Study 2

Colonial Elementary School

Terese Boegly

Authors' Note

Although there is much rhetoric about data-informed decision making, there are not many stories of the work that it takes to build data into instructional planning for students. The story that is told in this case study highlights a process of transforming a culture from using anecdotal information about students into using assessment data in a powerful way to improve student learning. As we all know about elementary school life, it is not easy for teachers to find the time to address both assessment and curriculum concerns. Notice how Boegly's innovations in terms of the use of time and accountability that teachers have to one another as well as to the students builds a dedicated learning community.

ABOVE AND BEYOND: A STORY OF SCHOOL IMPROVEMENT

Colonial School District (CSD) is located in Plymouth Meeting, Pennsylvania, a town just west of Philadelphia. The district enrollment is approximately 4,500 students. Colonial School District is comprised of one high school, one middle school, and five elementary schools.

Superintendent Dr. Vincent F. Cotter began his tenure during a troubled period in which a merit-based pay-for-performance initiative was being instituted. This was strongly opposed by the teachers' union. All constituents involved in the process of negotiating the teachers' contract knew it was critical for Colonial School District to develop a plan for improving student performance that was based on collaboration throughout the organization. In order to both address the concerns that were raised around this issue, as well as institute a system that would improve performance through professional collaboration, a problem solving group comprised of teachers and administrators came together. Under the leadership of the superintendent, the "Above and Beyond" plan was carefully developed which clearly identified the following eight steps for improvement:

1. Develop a District Vision and Belief System
2. Align Curriculum with Standards
3. Create a System of Assessment
4. Develop a Focused Staff Development Program
5. Raise Expectations for Learning for Students
6. Review Policies and Procedures and Their Respective Impact on Student Achievement
7. Create an Atmosphere of Pride and Responsibility
8. Create an Environment of Continuous Professional Development

This Above and Beyond plan led the way for a new form of governance in the district. A district improvement team was established which included principal, teacher, and central office representation. The purpose of this team was to review and monitor district and building goals. In addition, the district improvement team reviewed the allocation of the monetary awards that were given to each building for achieving the academic goals each year.

Each building formed its own school improvement team consisting of administrators and teachers. The building team developed goals in three areas: (a) improved student achievement, (b) use of technology, and (c) improved climate. Each year a $200,000 award was made available by the Colonial School Board, which was distributed among those schools. Funds were distributed using a formula that included a base award for each school and additional money for the successful attainment of each goal. The following criteria was established for developing the school improvement plans:

- Every building must use data in making instructional decisions.
- Every teacher must have the skills to work with data successfully.
- Curriculum and assessment data will be used to make critical decisions.
- Every building must have a School Improvement Plan.
- The goals and action plans contained in the building school improvement plan must be aligned with district goals and must include academic goals in math, reading, and writing.
- Each school must have a plan for data utilization and analysis.

In addition to goal setting, promoting teacher leadership and developing career development pathways within the district was a priority. Teachers were provided an opportunity to be identified as a master teacher. There was a competitive application process that included the submission of a portfolio as well as a demonstration lesson that was observed by a small team of teachers and administrators on the district improvement team. Designation as a master teacher was finalized by the superintendent. The position was designated for one school year at a time and included an additional $5,000 salary increment.

Curriculum development aligned with state and national standards has been based on Heidi Hayes-Jacobs' curriculum mapping work (1997) as well as Wiggins and McTighe's *Understanding by Design* (1998). Curriculum teacher leaders received extensive professional development and as their expertise solidified, they provided coaching and mentoring support to colleagues in the development of standards-based units of study and benchmark assessments. The CSD Teaching Standards, based on Charlotte Danielson's *Frameworks for Teaching* (1996), was jointly developed by teachers and administrators to establish consistent and clear expectations for teaching and learning across buildings and grade levels.

Implementation of the curriculum was supported by elementary and secondary math and reading coaches. Classroom teachers benefited from job-embedded professional development via co-planning, co-teaching, and reflective practice activities. The district has demonstrated its commitment to the establishment of a collaborative culture by providing teachers with additional common grade-level planning periods each week. In addition, personnel resources have been aligned to support coaching and co-teaching practices in the district. Teacher leaders hold study group sessions regularly with their colleagues to evaluate instructional needs, plan professional development sessions on topics such as formative assessment and differentiating instruction. They share effective teaching strategies, review current pedagogy, monitor at-risk students, and sharpen their focus on best practices in grading and assessment. Tiered professional development sessions for using reports from Performance Pathways, the technology we chose for tracking our assessment data, offered both administrators and teachers opportunities to discuss ways to improve student learning across standards and content areas.

Professional development to support teachers' use of technology to facilitate differentiated instruction, collaboration, and inquiry-based instruction has been ongoing in the Colonial School District. Teachers develop best practice lessons and share them with their colleagues using the technology available (i.e., Smart Board, document cameras, Safari/ Montage, United Streaming, Nettreckker DI, and digitized primary documents). Teachers' expertise using various technology tools has resulted in lessons that develop the students' ability to construct knowledge using twenty-first century skills, collaboratively solve real-world problems, and produce creative works.

A secondary instructional strategies coaching model was implemented and onsite university course work was offered to support elementary teacher needs for math and science content knowledge as well as K–12 support for enhancing writing instruction. In addition to enhancing the district's new teacher induction plan, differentiated professional development models were established for elementary and secondary teachers. Elementary teachers receive in-depth training and support regarding math and language arts literacy curriculum while new secondary teachers focus on management and instructional methodologies.

The impact made by curriculum standardization and a comprehensive system of assessment and professional development has been documented with increased student achievement scores on the state assessments in both whole school populations and in disaggregated groups.

The story that follows is a micro view of an elementary school from within the Colonial School District school system.

COLONIAL ELEMENTARY SCHOOL: USING A ZOOM LENS

Colonial Elementary School is a district-wide fourth and fifth grade elementary school. There are approximately 700 students in the school. The configuration at each grade level has been fairly consistent for a number of years. There are 15 sections of fourth grade and 15 sections of fifth grade. Colonial Elementary School also provides a continuum of special education to support students with various learning disabilities and special needs. Colonial Elementary School is a targeted Title 1 school. Colonial Elementary School has made significant gains in the area of mathematics and reading as measured by the Pennsylvania System of State Assessment (PSSA). These gains have been a result of ongoing data analysis, strategic curricular decisions, staff development, and modifications in instructional grouping practices.

Teacher leadership is very important in the Colonial School District and is strongly supported through many innovative initiatives. Teachers serve as department chairs, curriculum liaisons, reading specialists/coaches, and math coaches. These members of the professional staff are highly valued for their contributions in the area of curriculum, assessment, and staff development. They are very involved in the development, refinement, and revision of curriculum and assessment in the Colonial School District. In addition, these front line professionals serve as role models for their peers in the area of data analysis and application.

BUILDING PRINCIPAL AS THE MODEL FOR DATA ANALYSIS

As a building principal, it is important to recognize the power of the position, particularly when it comes to modeling for your professional staff what it is you expect from them. This could not be more important than in the area of data collection, analysis, and data driven decision-making. Prior to Colonial School District implementing the use of a highly effective software program, Performance Pathways, collecting and organizing data to share with the teachers took a considerable amount of time and effort. When Performance Pathways was implemented in the Colonial School District, learning to utilize the Web-based program was a priority. Modeling data-driven decision-making skills for the teachers was critical for having them begin to appreciate and recognize the importance of using assessment data in their professional practice.

Table 6.1 is a summary of the goals from the School Improvement Plan designed to develop teachers incorporate the use of technology to make instructional decisions regarding student achievement accurately and efficiently.

Table 6.1   School Improvement Plan Summary

School Year	Goal Statement	Action Plan
2003	Assessment data will be collected and utilized for instruction	• Staff development session and follow up sessions on data collection and record keeping • Create a database for collecting, posting, and sharing data
2004	Technology will be incorporated to make instructional decisions	• Staff development on Interpreting assessment data on Performance Pathways for state and national assessments • Create common local assessments for math and reading • Upload local assessments to Assessment Builder
2005	Utilize Performance Pathways to analyze student progress and teachers make informed instructional decisions to differentiate instruction based upon benchmark and local assessment data	• Upload revised benchmark and local assessments to Performance Pathways • Provide staff development to teachers on various report features on Performance Pathways • Schedule monthly coverage for teachers to collaborative review assessment data and create plans based upon their analysis • Provide staff development on differentiated instruction to further meet individual instructional needs of the students

FIRST FACULTY MEETING OF THE YEAR: REFLECT ON THE PAST AND PLAN FOR THE FUTURE

At the opening faculty meeting in August, teachers receive data profiles of their prior and current year students' performance on state and local assessments. Through careful reflection and analysis, teachers are able to identify areas of strength and need based upon this data. The data profile on their incoming students assists them in targeting priorities and differentiating instruction from the start of the school year. When the data is shared, teachers are asked to reflect upon the previous year's assessment data and look for trends and areas of strengths, as well as areas of growth. They are asked to honestly reflect (in private) if they felt they could improve the delivery of the curriculum or instruction in any area as it related to their previous year's class performance. For example, did they note that in the area of "literary devices" the students didn't do as well as non-fiction text features?

Grade-level data is also shared with the teachers. This data reveals by standard or reporting category how the grade level has done. This information is also critical for identifying grade-level strengths and needs. The identification of these trends helps provide some preliminary information for the school improvement team as they begin writing the school improvement plan. By sharing the grade-level assessment data prior to the teachers analyzing their own classroom data, there is an opportunity to model for the teachers how to effectively look at their data. It is always clearly articulated that this is only one piece of data. The data they will be collecting and analyzing through classroom observation, anecdotal records, and formative assessment will prove much more meaningful in their instructional decision making than the standardized, summative information they look at in the beginning of the year.

This exercise in data analysis has proven to be extremely valuable for the professional staff. The use of analytic reports from technology has made this process of data analysis a very manageable task as a building administrator. The assessment data is shared in a collegial and professional manner and there is no finger pointing or blame for the data. The teachers reflect privately and are encouraged to identify their own strengths and areas of need in order to address the issues identified.

GETTING READY FOR THE NEW SCHOOL YEAR: THE DATA PIPELINE

The job of the building principal is vast and varied. Day to day responsibilities and responding to, "Got a minute?" can take up the majority of the day. That is why it is critical to create and define a "data pipeline" before teachers come back each new school year. The following questions can provide direction in developing a pathway for the data:

- What common instructional assessments will be given during the school year? Who will be responsible for collecting the assessment data? Will it be curriculum supervisors, math coaches, or reading specialist?
- How can time be provided to the teachers and coaches to thoughtfully analyze their assessment data?
- How will you share this information back with the staff? Will it be analyzed for the teachers or will they do this independently or with their peers?
- Will the instructional coaches review the data with the classroom teachers?
- Will the curriculum supervisors come to a faculty meeting and give an overview?
- What do you expect your teachers to do with the data after they receive it?
- Will you be looking for strategic remediation or flexible grouping?

Developing a plan for disseminating assessment data and then providing the teachers with time to analyze the information is necessary for creating a culture and the expectation for data-driven decision making.

The key ingredients that I have found to help me lead with data are:

- Serve as a role model. Be interested in data, learn how to use the technology, identify with the teachers' need for support, and show how you value data analysis as a way to inform decisions.
- Provide a clear and explicit improvement plan that shows the expectations for the use of the technology and its data based reports.
- Create opportunities for teachers to collaborate and give meaning to the data.
- Sustain the effort over time. This will never happen in one school year!

THE USE OF REFLECTION TO FOSTER LEARNING

Prior to each mathematical unit of study, the teachers give a pre-assessment to determine what concepts and skills the students already know prior to the beginning of the unit. Colonial Elementary School follows a curriculum pacing calendar that identifies skills and concepts and the approximate time they should be taught and assessed throughout the school year. This calendar allows the math resource teachers to strategically support teachers and students throughout the school year. Teachers complete a reflective questionnaire for each math pre-assessment and forward the information to the principal.

Reflective Questions for Math Pre-Assessments

Please complete and send a copy along with pretest scores to TC ASAP–Thanks!

Identify the skills, concepts, or strategies where your students show strength and where they have weaknesses.

Which students do you foresee needing enrichment?

Which students do you foresee needing additional support and time learning concepts?

How can the Math Resource Teacher be helpful? (co-teaching, additional materials, resources, center development, incorporating process skills, etc.)

Formative assessment is essential for monitoring student progress. What concepts or skills would you like additional assessment activities, quick checks, ticket in/ ticket out, etc…?

Additional comments:

The information from this questionnaire is then passed on to the math resource teachers who analyze the information and work with the classroom teachers to address the identified needs and strengths. I could allow this information to go directly to the math resource/coach. However, I truly recognize that the classroom teachers are very busy and have many conflicting priorities. When information is requested by the building principal, it becomes a priority to the classroom teacher as well.

By reviewing this information, I continue to make the message clear, that this is important and worthy of a teacher's time.

CREATING TIME FOR DATA ANALYSIS: BUDDY SCHEDULE

Nothing is more important than creating time for teachers to collaborate and analyze assessment data together. One successful strategy is the "Buddy Schedule." The Buddy Schedule pairs two classroom teachers from two different grade levels. All fourth grade teachers have a "buddy classroom" in fifth grade. Each month release time is scheduled for either the entire grade level or grade-level team. During Buddy Scheduling, the entire class reports to their buddy classroom, packed for dismissal, with independent reading book in hand. Students are expected to read quietly around the classroom while the buddy classroom completes their instruction for the day. In the event there may be a discipline concern, special accommodations with the guidance counselor or support staff are made for that student.

Buddy Schedule
3:00–3:50 p.m. Coverage

Please use this coverage schedule when an entire grade level is going to meet at 3:10. Please have your students packed up with an independent reading book in hand. Be sure to review classroom buddy visitor expectations with your students. If you have any concerns regarding a student who may need some additional supervision, please contact the guidance counselor for special arrangements.

Cluster D Teachers	Cluster A Teachers
Rosen, Niki 302	Corba, Melissa 201
Moyer, Alison 303	Cash, Roe 202
Forst, Jay 305	Carbondale, Nick 213
McDonald, Mike 325	Smithston, Kim 216
Childs, LInda 327	Marks, Joe 217

Buddy Schedule provides the opportunity for teachers to meet and collaboratively score or analyze data from a benchmark assessment. In addition, this schedule is used on a smaller scale to run new teacher meetings to provide support or staff development. This schedule has been very well received by the teachers and they truly appreciate the time they receive for collaboration. Although this schedule does not meet all the needs of the teachers with regards to data analysis, it does provide some support and once again reinforces the message that data-driven decision making is critical to student success.

In addition to the Buddy Schedule, collaborative time for planning and instruction are part of the regular instructional schedule for classroom teachers. Teams of teachers coplan and coteach with both the reading and math specialists on a weekly basis. Some teachers, based on need or experience, are provided additional support.

The key ingredients that I have found to help me lead with data are:

- Serve as a role model. Be interested in data, learn how to use the technology, identify with the teachers' need for support, and show how you value data analysis as a way to inform decisions.
- Provide a clear and explicit improvement plan that shows the expectations for the use of the technology and its data-based reports.
- Create opportunities for teachers to collaborate and give meaning to the data.
- Sustain the effort over time. This will never happen in one school year!

COLONIAL SCHOOL DISTRICT: USING A WIDE ANGLE LENS

The success of this work is realized in student growth in learning. Figures 6.1 and 6.2 illustrate the results at Colonial Elementary School from 2001–2007.

Figure 6.1 Data collected from 2001 through 2007 reveals notable increases in student achievement at all grade levels.

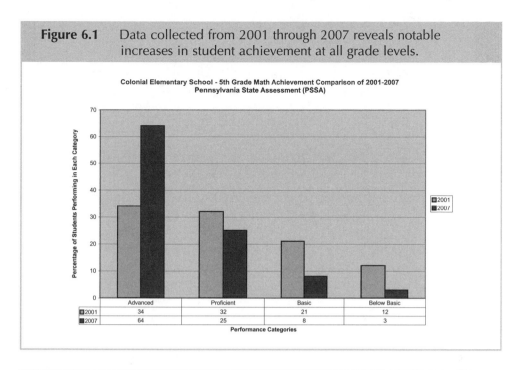

Colonial Elementary School - 5th Grade Math Achievement Comparison of 2001-2007
Pennsylvania State Assessment (PSSA)

	Advanced	Proficient	Basic	Below Basic
2001	34	32	21	12
2007	64	25	8	3

Performance Categories

Figure 6.2 Achievement for students included in disaggregate groups has been remarkable when comparing proficiency levels from 2001 to 2007. PSSA results revealed all targeted groups in Colonial School District made AYP.

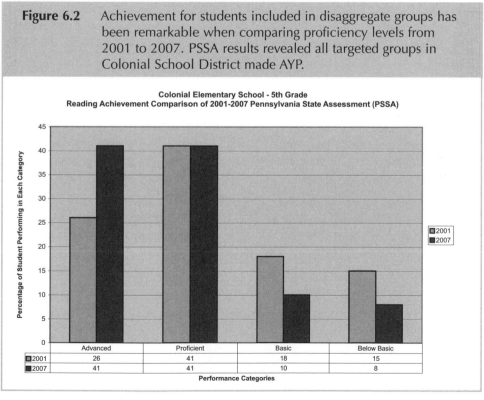

Colonial Elementary School - 5th Grade
Reading Achievement Comparison of 2001-2007 Pennsylvania State Assessment (PSSA)

	Advanced	Proficient	Basic	Below Basic
2001	26	41	18	15
2007	41	41	10	8

Performance Categories

7 Case Study 3

West Chester East High School

Richard F. Dunlap Jr.

Authors' Note

This case study provides some insight into a frequently asked question—how can we bring about change at the secondary level? Rick Dunlap provides important insights into how he worked to change the culture of the school as he built community, trust, and distributed teacher leadership. Perhaps one of the most powerful lessons described in this case study is that it takes time to transform a culture.

A HIGH SCHOOL JOURNEY: FROM INDIVIDUAL TO COHESIVE CURRICULUM

When I first became the principal of West Chester East High School in 2002, one of the tasks we were trying to accomplish was to revise curriculum in light of standards. The whole concept of a standards-based curriculum was starting to impact the high schools in our area. In February, Dr. Alan Elko, the superintendent of the West Chester Area School District, and Dr. Linda Antonowich, the assistant superintendent for curriculum, asked me to attend a Curriculum Mapping Institute to learn more about linking standards to curriculum revision.

Since the mapping institute was not going to take place until the summer, I had some time to ascertain the level of knowledge our staff at East High School had in relation to the curriculum mapping process. This time also gave me an opportunity to acquire some knowledge about the ideas and works presented at the institute: Heidi Hayes Jacobs, *Mapping the Big Picture* (1997); Grant Wiggins and Jay McTighe, *Understanding by Design* (1998); and Arthur L. Costa and Bena Kallick, *Habits of Mind* (2000). From the outset, I wanted to make certain that teachers were actively engaged in the revision of curriculum. The process started with the goal of linking standards to curriculum and evolved into a change in the way our school culture now operates.

In February 2002, we started planning. We had received a grant from the state of Pennsylvania to improve our state test scores. In a planning session with the department chairs, we allocated the grant to various aspects of school improvement. Some of the money was allocated to fund a team to attend the mapping institute. During a faculty meeting that spring, I read a short story to the faculty and led a discussion about changing the way we do things in order to work better as a team. I reminded the faculty that we needed to come up with a system that would permit us to link the state standards to our curriculum. The book, *Outlearning the Wolves: Surviving and Thriving in a Learning Organization* (Hutchens, 2000), was read out loud while I had the pictures in the story projected on to a screen. The use of this book as a teaching tool was very beneficial.

In short, *Outlearning the Wolves* is the story of an organization that might resemble your own place of work. Included in this place of work are bad habits, vulnerabilities, and resignation to the status quo. In a quote from the leaf of the book jacket, "A flock of sheep, fearful of the wolves' mythical cleverness, is initially debilitated by fragmentation and false assumptions. But as the sheep build a culture for learning, the contributions of each individual are utilized in striking new and productive ways." The compelling lesson for me in using this as a teaching tool was that 150 teachers were talking about the story for days following the meeting. This generated a shared experience to draw upon as we worked to make learning an integral part of our reform strategy.

YEAR ONE: A STARTING POINT

Following the faculty meeting, I asked if there were any teachers interested in going to Salt Lake City with me in the summer. I didn't share any more information other than it would be an all-expenses-paid trip, which included a conference that would enable us to continue working on linking the standards to our curriculum. Before I returned to my office, I had three teachers stop me and say that they were very interested in going to Utah. I asked them to meet me the next morning so I could talk with them about what we were intending to do on the trip. All three teachers were very excited about being able to go to a conference.

By the end of our meeting, we had a core team that was going to attend the institute.

Prior to leaving for the trip, we planned our own itinerary. Since we were relatively new to each other, the trip was planned in a fashion that allowed for each of us to plan an activity that would enable us to bond as a team. The activity could only take place when we were not required to be in attendance at the conference. This would become a standard strategy that would be utilized for all future overnight conferences. We attended the conference in July 2002. The conference gave us a starting point and allowed us to network with those who had experience with mapping. It gave us time to speak with others about their pitfalls, trials, and tribulations. We ended up designing our own professional development strategies for our faculty for the upcoming school year. This became a standard when attending future conferences. The evening activities that were planned by each member of the team were a benefit because we took each other out of our comfort zones, which enabled us to bond better as a team. For example, one night we went on a three-hour horseback ride and then attended a chuck wagon dinner, another night we went to a musical, and on one of the nights we hit a few historical sights. By doing these activities it enabled us to talk, bounce ideas off each other, share our daily experiences, and plan for the future. One of the special things that happened during this conference was that our team agreed to become a core training team for the rest of our building.

Sharing Our Findings

The team decided to show an overview PowerPoint presentation to the full faculty on the first day of school. This overview included a brief description of what we learned about the mapping process and included some building goals we felt were reasonable to accomplish in the first year. I sent a "welcome back to school" letter to the faculty, which included a homework assignment to be completed by the first faculty meeting. It was an article by Heidi Hayes Jacobs, titled *New Trends in Curriculum* (Jacobs, 2001), as well as responding to a short questionnaire, *What Is Useful Curriculum?* (Udelhofen, 2005), inquiring about our current curriculum guides.

What Is Useful Curriculum?

Directions: Nearly every district has some type of formal curriculum that is designed to guide instruction. These guides are usually comprised of large binders that are often too cumbersome and outdated to be useful in classroom instruction. It has been our experience that most teachers rarely refer to these guides. Instead, they rely on textbooks, supplemental materials and their personal preference to guide their instruction. In the fragmented curriculum that results, some important material may go untaught, while other material is repeated needlessly. To be meaningful and useful for meeting student needs, the curriculum must be an accessible tool that effectively guides instruction and is aligned both to standards and the curriculum of other grade levels.

Consider the curriculum you currently use to guide your instruction and compare it to the criteria listed in the chart on the following page (see Table 7.1).

The following curriculum sources guide my instruction (please list).

_____

_____

_____

_____

_____

_____

_____

_____

_____

Considering the curriculum sources you listed in the What Is Useful Curriculum? questionnaire, complete the following chart:

Table 7.1   Curriculum Needs Assessment Survey

Criteria The curriculum I currently used to guide instruction is	Yes	Somewhat	No	We Need
Highly visible and accessible to teachers, students, and parents				
Presented in a user-friendly format				
Easily and continually revised on a timely basis – based on teacher input, collaboration, and latest research				
A tool that is easy to use for new teachers – new to teaching or new to the district				
A tool that provides information about the skills that precede and follow a particular grade level or course				
At the core of teaching practice				
Clearly aligned with standards				
Your additions:				
Based on your analysis of the curriculum you currently use to guide instruction, what key areas need further attention to meet the needs of all students more effectively?				

When the teachers returned to school, they were given a written curriculum, if it was available, for each course of study he or she would be teaching for the upcoming school year. The article and questionnaire were discussed in a large group setting prior to seeing the Power Point presentation. The discussion was a good starting point for our staff. The assignment allowed them to reflect on some of their own educational practices in relation to the curriculum of the courses they were present-ing to our students. The presentation reinforced the ideas generated by the assignment and discussion. By the conclusion of the upcoming school year, each staff member was asked to construct a map for each course he or she was teaching. Each faculty member received a copy of the map template via email. The core team stressed the use of technology as a means of easily beginning and developing the map throughout the year. Also, I provided each department with a copy of Jacob's book, *Mapping the Big Picture* (1997). I asked each of our department chairs to read the book before next month's department chair meeting.

Introducing the Mapping Process

Our teachers have a great deal of respect for our department chairs. They rely on them for vital communications between both the building administration and central office administration. Our core committee decided that this would be a good starting point for introducing the mapping process. In my opinion, this low level leadership is one of the strongest assets available to any building principal. It is the closest to the action in every classroom. Teachers not only rely on department chairs for the basic needs in accomplishing their jobs (supplies and materials) but also for their knowledge in dealing with the daily challenges that teachers face. There is always dialogue in the teacher workrooms cen-tered on instruction, assessment, and curriculum. Our core team felt that if we trained the department chairs in the curriculum mapping process, and relied on both the leadership of the department chairs and the building principal, we would be able to tackle this concept and make it work as a cyclical process.

The team presented a second PowerPoint presentation to the faculty department chairpersons. The presentation also included discussion on reading *Mapping the Big Picture*. I instructed the department chairs to pay close attention to each of the slides in the presentation, for each one of them would be presenting these at next month's faculty meeting. The slides focused on the cycle of curriculum mapping, the differences among skills, content, and assessments within various curriculums. Hostility was blatant and questions were abundant:

- Why do we need to do this?
- This is too simplistic!
- Are we lowering the bar of a quality education?

Even though everyone understood the need for this kind of work, linking the standards to the curriculum through a format that was going to have us take a step back and go through a long, detailed, descriptive process. It gave the teachers a sense that we were biting off more than we could chew. The members of the core team gave the department chairs emphatic reassurances that this was accomplishable. An important point to mention here is that the three teachers who made up the core team with me had a tremendous amount of respect from the entire building. All three teachers were master teachers in their own right. Although the core team got their armor dented a little along the way, it was their belief in the curriculum mapping process, as well as my own, that helped us sustain the effort.

We all saw this as a way to put everyone on the same level playing field when working with curriculum, assessments, and instructional practices as well as aligning the standards to our courses. This factor alone allowed us to move through the process without getting skinned alive by the department chairs and the rest of the faculty. To this day, this factor still carries our initiative forward. An interesting point that continues to support and shape my style of leadership is that initiatives which include teachers, generated from the bottom-up instead of a top-down approach, have a lasting significance. The initiative is not another one of those things you do for one year and put it on the shelf. How often do we hear, in the business of education, "this too shall pass"? If teachers are an integral part of the process, it is not only accomplishable, but becomes a lasting practice.

Some of the ideas that came out of the meeting with the department chairs included encouraging them to finish reading *Mapping the Big Picture* and share it with the members of their department. Each department chair volunteered to present various slides of the same training PowerPoint presentation at the next faculty meeting. We discussed with them the goal of having each teacher in their department complete a month-to-month map for each course of instruction by May of the current school year. The meeting also included a planning session for a teacher in-service day that was going to occur in the later part of the fall. This in-service would also include a training session for the entire faculty, by the core team, on the benefits of mapping.

I started the October Faculty Meeting with a brief introduction on the curriculum mapping process. As soon as the first department chair jumped in on the presentation, the tenor of the meeting quickly changed. The teachers seemed to respond in a positive manner. They acknowledged that the use of mapping would eliminate repetition and omissions in the curriculum from middle school to high school. Everyone recognized that attaching the standards would be the difficult task. Some concerns arose about the district-created mid-term and final examinations. I addressed the concern with my hope for more autonomy in the district's philosophy of these assessment tools. [Note: Two years after we started the mapping process, the mid-term and final exams were abolished and teachers were permitted to develop quarterly assessments. These assessments are better linked to the instructional practices and the curriculum being delivered to our students.]

The smooth ride during the faculty meeting did hit some turbulence. Some of the negative comments that surfaced stated things like:

- "Mapping is the old scope and sequence."
- "Someone is making money on this."
- "Teachers used to be paid for curriculum development and NOW we are expected to do this for free."

Comments like these would be heard less and less as we progressed through the mapping process. Once the teachers, especially the old guard, gained a better understanding and saw the value in what we were doing, the resistance lessened. The upcoming teacher in-service day proved to be a strong link in keeping the endeavor alive. The core team was able to help the department chairs present mapping to the faculty. They trained others individually and provided materials to support the initiative. Their overall facilitation of the process encouraged the staff and they started a database of information that could be linked to technology.

In October 2002, the entire staff went to Camp Tockwogh in Maryland, about an hour and a half away from school. T-shirts were designed and distributed for all to wear with a logo and an inspirational design and saying related to a pack of wolves correlating to the story that was read to the faculty at a meeting the previous spring. An anxious faculty left a warm, cozy building to board yellow school buses in a downpour that lasted all day. On the ride, people interacted with others they usually didn't see on a daily basis and they enjoyed coffee and donuts. The day's agenda consisted of three activities:

- Team building activities
- An overview of the district's recent Strategic Plan
- The Association for Supervision and Curriculum Development (ASCD) video presentation on Curriculum Mapping

After each session, there was a brief period for questions and answers. Most feedback was positive as many gained a sense of comfort after they viewed the video, which provided a good overview and demonstrated the benefits of maps. Despite the weather, the warm buffet lunch was a big hit and the day, on the whole, was a success.

Although we felt we had offered the faculty a solid foundation to start constructing their own maps, there was still a cloud of anxiety. The cloud began to dissipate as we worked one-on-one with teachers, encouraging them to look at the models and to apply their own curriculum to the same format. The core team was a huge benefit to the school. They helped the department chairs cover more territory by assisting with one-on-one attention to individual teachers. The remainder of the school year in-service days as well as faculty meeting time were given to the faculty to enable them to complete their maps.

By May of that school year, every teacher completed and turned in a diary map for each course to the building principal. The maps were not part of the teacher evaluation system; however, the maps were evaluated by the principal, the department chairs, and the core team. Maps that did not provide sufficient detail were given back to the teacher with a request for revision before the end of the school year.

Reflecting on Year One

Looking back, our team concluded that we should have included the assistant principals from the start of this process. Including them would have enabled the systemic change to flow more freely. From that point on, the assistant principals became much more involved in the curriculum mapping process. By making sure the maps were clean and in good working order, the teachers would not be embarrassed by their individual work. Most important, with strong diary maps we could then move on to the next phase of the mapping process.

On a separate note, I had my first "Aha moment" at the end of this school year. An interesting phenomenon had occurred before the teachers left for the summer. We had a large number of our faculty retire. New teachers were being interviewed to replace the staff lost due to retirement. In addition, many of the existing staff were going to be changing the courses and levels of courses that they were currently teaching for the upcoming school year. Many of the teachers that were changing their assignments asked me for a copy of the diary maps, which were developed over the past year. They wanted to review the curriculum maps prior to the start of the new school year and work from existing maps. For the sake of the journey, this was a huge benefit. This was one of those moments when I first realized that this process was starting to take hold and from the faculty's perspective there was a sense of worth in what we were doing with mapping. It was the first time many teachers had a written curriculum and they were able to see connections across the disciplines.

CONTINUING THE PROCESS: YEAR TWO

The second year of the journey we added two more members to the core team, and they joined the original team the following summer in

Utah at the Mapping Institute. An interesting aspect that added to the professional development of the core team was that we would be presenting at the conference. Presenting at the conference was a way for our core team to stay up-to-date with the different aspects of mapping, make connections with others, receive new training, and better understand the mapping process.

Our core team trained all new teachers by developing a training model that was implemented in after school sessions. The new teachers received training on how to create their own diary maps and how to work with the core maps we developed for each course of study. We made our goals manageable and realistic, especially since we were anticipating there would be a job action by our teacher's association. In the fall of our second year of mapping, the teachers went on strike. This put a hold on what we expected we could accomplish for the year. The strike ended after thirteen days. However, we, as a faculty, decided that it would be better to take a break from the mapping process until we could let the dust settle due to the negative feelings after the job action. We did not resume mapping until February of the second school year.

However, we picked up the process of mapping seamlessly as if we had never taken a break. Some department supervisors started unpacking the standards for certain curricular areas and the department chairs, along with the core team, started to develop what we referred to as "consensus maps." At the present time, our consensus maps have become what are now called "Core Curriculum." Through the use of in-service days, department meeting times, and faculty meetings, we were able to carve out time to complete this segment of the process. This part of the process enabled us to have an agreement or consensus on the core curriculum for each course of study and to include the different levels as well. It also became a practice for us to use faculty meetings in a different format. Instead of having faculty meetings that were house-keeping agendas, where administrators shared information, they turned into mini work sessions. The dialogue and curriculum sharing that occurred during this time was much more productive to our school and the mapping process than the old-fashioned type of faculty meeting. Every now and then we have a typical meeting, but for the most part the standard format for faculty meetings has changed. All information in the sense of house keeping types of items is now shared through email with the staff.

Again, at the close of the school year, teachers clamored for the consensus maps in the areas they would be teaching for the upcoming school year. We followed the same process of evaluating the consensus maps as we did for the diary maps. The department chairs, core team, and the building principal reviewed the maps. If any maps were not written to the acceptable standard, the map was returned to the group of teachers who developed the map. They completed the map before they signed out for the summer break.

A DIFFERENT PERSPECTIVE: YEAR THREE

Before we headed back to the Mapping Institute for the third year, we added two more members to our core team. We now had representative membership in the core for the different subject areas in the building. Again, our core team presented at the Institute on what we had accomplished over the past two years. Our core team was able to stay sharp by presenting, attending many of the sessions, and networking with other professionals. In addition to presenting, they had complete run of the conference. Their goal was to attend as many sessions as they could and absorb as much information as they could. One of the benefits in doing this with the new teachers attending the conference was the idea of letting teachers have time to attend training sessions without any other responsibilities. Their goal was to enjoy the conference, participate in the activities that the core team planned during the off hours, and to relax.

Over the years I have heard some sort of language from every teacher who attended the conference about the rejuvenation of their motivation toward teaching. Our core team really spent some time in developing quality activities for our group in the evenings. We visited many historical sites, went white water rafting, horseback riding, four wheeling, and shopping. As a team attending the conference, we participated in every activity the conference hosted. One year we won the top song parody contest in every category. Many of the door prizes were free conference tuitions and literature by current authors. Winning those contests enabled us to bring more people to the conference the following year. The best time, and meaningful in many ways, was the time we had together in the form of socializing and eating in nice restaurants in the evenings. We all were able to learn about each other and our families. Most of all, we were able to continue planning the staff development for the next school year.

The journey moved into the third year with a whole different perspective on what was to be accomplished. In keeping in line with the process, we continued to train the new staff. Two of the big objectives that we had for the third year were to accomplish both small group reviews and a large group review. After developing consensus maps, the core team and the department chairs felt that we had accumulated enough information to divide the faculty up into small groups and conduct a small group review of the curriculum. The faculty was divided up into fifteen teams with six members and two co-facilitators per group. The aligning of these small groups was done strategically with the help of the core team, assistant principals, and the department chairs. The reason for purposefully designing each team was to separate the negative people and ensure the success of the groups. Some of the more negative people toward the idea of curriculum mapping were chosen as facilitators. This strategy proved to be highly successful. It gave the process more clout, and for the first time in a long while, the small group reviews created a forum for dialogue among the faculty.

For a whole in-service day, our teachers went through two small group reviews. The first small group review was completed by each department chair with his or her respective department. The afternoon session was led by the co-facilitators with a mixed group of teachers. The teachers were from different departments and the groups were set up so one department could not dominate the group. Both small group reviews generated discussion from a series of posing questions designed to stimulate dialogue among the teachers. The afternoon session required the groups to complete a T-Chart based on their group's dialogue. The information was collected by the core team members when each group finished their work. An interesting point as a result of the small group reviews was that although our school day ended at 3:00 p.m., at 5:00 p.m. we were still collecting work from the small groups. It was not because the work was so demanding and it needed a large amount of time to complete the task. Rather, it was because everyone was so engaged in meaningful discussions facilitated by the co-leaders.

I am a firm believer in teacher leadership. The success of this endeavor can be measured by the number of times the teacher leadership positions in the building had an active part in the curriculum mapping process. The success of the small group review happened because of the core team, the facilitators, and the department chairs.

Following the small group reviews, the core team assembled together with the building principal to analyze the information created by the small groups. The information was cataloged into usable data that would enable the building principal to conduct a large group review. The information was condensed into a one-page handout that was distributed at a faculty meeting. The building principal went through a large group review at the same faculty meeting. As we went through the large group review, the teachers acknowledged that by reading others' maps they had gained a new awareness of information about what other teachers were trying to accomplish. It was here that a second "Aha moment" had occurred for me. Teachers voiced the realization that they all taught similar skills embedded in the content of their discipline. From these conversations we learned:

- Where the gaps and repetitions were in our curriculum
- How we might merge concepts from two or more disciplines
- How we might take a whole new approach to literacy
- How we could start a ninth grade academy for students who needed a better introduction to high school

Throughout the entire large group review we looked for patterns. Some pieces of information were given to specific groups to deal with so that they could overcome barriers that affected their departments. An example of this is when it was discovered that the math department taught the concept of plotting points on a graphing calculator in the spring of the tenth grade year, yet the science department required the students to be able to use this as a skill in the fall of the tenth grade year. Through a collaborative effort between the two departments the science department decided they would teach the skill in their chemistry course and the math department would review the concept knowing that this represented an overlap between the two courses. The math department would take the skill deeper into the content of the course. This also turned out to be an opportunity for integrating the curriculum.

Sharing What We Learned

Around this time, the efforts of our mapping experience were not only being noticed by the leaders of our own school district, but they were being noticed by the leadership of surrounding school districts. During the course of this school year, our core team went on the road to train the leaders of a local school district in the process of curriculum mapping, as well as the teachers and administrators of another local high school. We had the opportunity to work in partnership with a local state educational association known as an Intermediate Unit or I.U. They asked our core team to present at a workshop for the administrative leaders of all the school districts in our county. We were able to co-present with Bena Kallick, who was the keynote speaker for the event. This workshop made the other school districts aware of the work in curriculum the folks at West Chester East High School were doing.

In addition, this workshop served as the catalyst we were looking for to incorporate technology into our process. Since we started our journey, we were looking for a way to utilize technology to make this process more dynamic and user friendly. Our district management team was able to view software and, through the leadership of our superintendent, we were able to break down any walls of resistance about using technology for this purpose. The superintendent saw the advantages of teacher leadership and decided to support the mapping initiative for the entire district. This was an important juncture for our journey.

Sustaining the Initiative

When working in a large school district there are many different leaders working on many different initiatives. At this time our district had two high schools, three middle schools, and ten elementary schools. We have added another high school since we started the journey. We had a large central office staff that included supervisors for every subject area, and a large cabinet made up of directors and assistant superintendents. As a building principal, it was very difficult to continue building initiatives because there was always another initiative being started by someone in a position of authority. It seemed to me that it was very difficult to accomplish anything because so many different things were going on. I knew the teachers were getting frustrated with the many different directives. As educators, we have been known to ask ourselves, "What do we take off of our plate so we can add the new initiative?" How many times do we hear educators saying things like, "Just go through the motions, it will go away and come back before you retire."

For some reason our building was able to defy the odds and sustain this initiative to make it worthwhile for the teachers and, more important, for the students. The most important factor was that this initiative became ingrained into the daily life of our teaching staff. Since the start of our journey, our superintendent pared the central office staff down, increased the building-level leadership, and created a curriculum council made up of the building administrators. The building-level administrators are known as liaisons to specifically assigned areas of curriculum.

We want to make certain that this initiative will be sustained regardless of changes in the leadership. Over the past year, the core team and the teachers in the building were driving this work. Many people always said that if I were to leave, this initiative would die. I began to feel that it would not go away because of the core team and the department chairs. As a building principal, you are involved in many different aspects of a high school. The core team kept the focus on this initiative. They made suggestions, developed models, created PowerPoint presentations, held core team meetings, planned professional development workshops, worked with individual teachers, and took this initiative by the horns and continued to lead our faculty through the process. I found myself not getting further away from the process, but relinquishing the idea of being the point person with the mapping process. I can honestly say that this initiative has incorporated everyone's voice. All of the stakeholders, the teachers of East High School, have a say in the process.

TEACHING LITERACY: YEAR FOUR

Year four of the journey started out with us training the new teachers, moving from consensus maps to core maps, and we added a new feature to the mapping process. We incorporated the idea of literacy across the curriculum into the mapping process. The beauty of using the mapping process as an overarching umbrella is that it enables a teacher to incorporate many different initiatives. Many times the other initiatives seemed fragmented and they often did not link with the other things that were going on in the classroom or the building. The process of curriculum mapping provided our building with a tool for synthesizing the different initiatives to improve student learning. A good example of this occurred for us during our fourth year. We were starting a significant literacy effort that was to transcend into each classroom. The discussion and ideas presented during the large group review process were able to be organized in a fashion that all teachers would be teachers of literacy. We started a core literacy team that trained at the University of Pennsylvania's Literacy Academy and in the Reading Apprenticeship program.

The core literacy team was made up members who were not on the core mapping team. Again, more leadership started to exert itself in the building. The core literacy team wanted to focus on teaching literacy skills in all classrooms. The idea of teaching reading, writing, speaking, and listening skills did not just fall on the English teachers. The core literacy team reached out and used the mapping process. Not only did they function with the department chairs in providing staff development to the teachers in literacy, they also worked with the mapping core team. During this year, the English literacy standards were identified and labeled on everyone's diary map as well as the core maps. This was an important breakthrough for us. We held in-service workshops and used faculty meetings as staff development sessions like the mapping team did in making literacy across the curriculum impact students in all classes. During a faculty meeting time being used as a workshop session, it was nice to hear a science teacher of thirty years talk to the faculty about how he taught reading, not just biology. The literacy effort has incorporated writing strategies that are taught in all classrooms.

Music to my ears occurred when I had a teacher email at the end of one day. She informed me that one of her students responded to her directions when she told the class to complete a Type I writing assignment at the beginning of her class. The student said this was the fifth Type I writing assignment he did that day! The literacy effort was taking hold and becoming a way of life through the mapping process. The teachers felt the worth and saw where it was happening in the curriculum they were delivering through instruction and assessment. Another aspect of the literacy effort was strengthened through the mapping process. When the teachers had time to review their maps and look for gaps and overlaps with the skills they associated with the literacy standards, they started to realize they were asking the students to use different literacy skills when learning the content than they were when they assessed the students. Small group reviews within the department and across the curriculum enabled teachers to put more clarity in their efforts with literacy.

Some of our health teachers started to implement the developmental series, *Habits of Mind* (Costa & Kallick, 2000), into their daily teaching practices. Our health department chair had a big influence on the rest of the department with this initiative. It linked very well with the mapping process. These thinking skills and lifelong learning habits are well documented in their diary maps. This was another example of leadership on the teacher level. Here is an initiative that became a sustained practice because there was time to develop the theory into a practice that has meaning. Both students and teachers grew from this experience.

When Heidi Hayes Jacobs asked us to participate with the Association of Supervision and Curriculum Development (ASCD) in the development of her new video series, we were honored. To be featured in one of her videos added a lot of clout to what we were doing. There was even more acceptance by the staff and the district administration. The core team really became motivated and excited with the video product. Other people were featured with the work they were doing in the classroom as a result of the mapping experience. Many of these people were not department chairs or members of the core team. There were even a few people who did not work in the building, but did work in the district who were featured. The video experience strengthened and validated the work we were doing. It was also a valuable learning experience for not only the teachers but also for our students. Students from our communications classes worked side by side with the directors and the ASCD film crew. This experience also had an effect on the members of our staff. It gave them a sense of pride in the work they were doing. The mapping process was not going away and the journey would continue.

MOVING FORWARD: YEAR FIVE

The journey entered its fifth year with the pleasure of knowing that we finally had the technology we wanted so badly. The notion that this process was not going away was now becoming a reality. Not only did the technology strengthen this idea, but so did the superintendent with his next move. Following our return from attending and presenting at the Mapping Institute for the fifth year, the superintendent asked for our core team to do a presentation of what had occurred at West Chester East High School over the last five years to all of the administrators of the other two high schools. In August 2006, we presented to those administrators with the help of a representative from Performance Pathways. The other schools were directed to look at what had been accomplished at East and asked to come up with a way to link standards to the curriculum and ensure that the curriculum at their school was the same curriculum being delivered at the other two high schools.

The journey was moving forward. The superintendent gave everyone one month to come up with a way to build a core curriculum in their buildings. Rather than reinvent the wheel, the other schools quickly joined in on learning the process of using curriculum mapping as the tool. The use of technology was going to make this a much easier process for the other schools. It was clearly defined by the superintendent that the core maps developed at East were a starting point for the members of each department to come together and collaborate on developing core maps for the West Chester Area School District. The superintendent charged the building leaders with a deadline on making sure the core maps were completed and linked to the standards by June 2008.

Our core team was becoming a training team for the rest of the district. They worked as consultants to one of our middle schools. Our feeder middle school was the first school to contact our team and ask for their help in starting the process. The journey definitely picked up speed and a greater sense of longevity. The core team even developed their own Web site to supplement the professional development training workshops and as a resource for others involved in the practice of curriculum mapping.

Another thing that helped the other high schools to utilize the curriculum mapping process was the College Board's Advanced Placement Audit. All of the AP courses were to be submitted to the College Board for approval by January of this year. The liaisons and supervisors were charged with making sure this task was complete. The core maps from East were the starting point for the teachers of the AP classes. Looking back on when we first started this process, I was glad we decided to map every course at every level the first year we started the journey. We felt at that time that we were biting off more than we could chew; however, the benefit of having all of the courses mapped outweighed the short term convenience of mapping the building's courses in some sort of segmented fashion.

REFLECTING ON THE JOURNEY

As I look back on this journey, I can see all of the different paths that were blazed by the teachers. Their leadership, professionalism, and commitment to a process that has value have taken root. I believe in the mapping process. It puts the curriculum in the hands of the teacher on a daily basis, not on a shelf. One of the biggest benefits of the mapping process, with the use of technology and the data a teacher has at his or her fingertips, is the ability to create, deliver, and assess instruction in a differentiated way that makes it easier to reach the student on an individual basis.

The words in this essay reflect my perception of what has transpired at West Chester East High School; however, they acknowledge the hard work of the following individuals on our core team: Dr. Eileen Riley, Linda Miller, Dr. Mary Beans, Deb Sabatino, Beth Ann Carozza, Eric Bucci, Tracy Heim, Joe Arscott, Scott Rafetto, Julie Robertson, and

Vicki Croul. Any one of them could have authored this essay. In a larger sense, they did, in fact, write the journey.

The journey continues . . . .

8 Tips for Staying the Course

It is often easy enough to get started. There is energy and excitement about what you hope will be a real shift in the way you are working. You hope to improve the organization so that it can provide the best opportunities for student learning. There is momentum. You have also included in your vision where you would like to end. You have stated your outcomes and you know where the map should end. What you are now facing is the hard part—getting through the middle! As you already know, change is inevitable and this includes unforeseen changes that will inevitably occur along the way. For example, there may be a new superintendent, there may be a new direction from the Board of Education, building principals may change, and teachers will retire. In addition to personnel changes, there are likely to be changes based on the social and political environment in which schools reside. So, how do you stay the course?

1. Distribute the leadership. Do not depend on any one or two individuals to do the work.
2. Seek new leaders. Find where the expertise is. Do not depend on position to determine who your leaders are.
3. Provide clear communications about what you are doing. Educate your Board of Education, parents, and community.
4. Celebrate your successes, and learn from your mistakes.
5. Use a feedback spiral for continuous growth and improvement.
6. Always pay attention to learning—student learning, teacher learning, organizational learning. Do not lose sight of your organization as a learning organization.
7. Stay current with new trends and research from the field.

8. Stay current with the action research that is possible within your own organization.
9. Use consultants cautiously and wisely. Make sure that consultants know your action plan and see where their work fits in with what you are doing.
10. Make certain that you are moving forward and that you are not holding on to ineffective practices.

Keep revisiting your framework:

1. Is the vision what you mean it to be? If not, how should it change? If so, how well are you moving toward realizing the vision?
2. Is your staff skillful enough to work within the vision? What more can you do to make certain that the skills you have identified are learned? What new skills need to be addressed?
3. Do you have the proper incentives for your staff? How might that change?
4. Are the resources in place? If not, what is needed at this point?
5. Is your action plan adequately monitored? If not, what might you do about it?

Collins (2001) describes the phase for sustaining organizational change with these caveats:

Clock Building, Not Time Telling

Truly great organizations prosper through multiple generations of leaders, the exact opposite of being built around a single great leader, great idea, or specific program. Leaders in great organizations build catalytic mechanisms to stimulate progress, and do not depend upon having a charismatic personality to get things done; indeed, many had a "charisma bypass."

Preserve the Core and Stimulate Progress

Enduring great organizations are characterized by a fundamental duality. On the one hand, they have a set of timeless core values and a core reason for being that remain constant over long periods of time. On the other hand, they have a relentless drive for change and progress—a creative compulsion that often manifests in BHAGs (Big Hairy Audacious Goals). Great organizations keep clear the difference between their core values (which never change) and operating strategies and cultural practices (which endlessly adapt to a changing world) (Collins, 2001, p. 35).

Our advice? Map your way to success and stay the course, riding each wave and turbulence as a problem to be solved rather than a barrier that prevents continuing the journey.

References

Ainsworth, L. (2003). *Power standards: Identifying the standards that matter the most.* Englewood, CO: Advanced Learning Press.

Ambrose, D. (1996). Turtle soup: Establishing innovation-friendly conditions for school reform. *Journal of Creative Behavior, (30)*1, pp. 25–38.

Budan, K. (2006). Unpublished paper written for Performance Pathways, Mechanicsburg, PA.

Collins, J. (2001). *Good to great: Why some companies make the leap . . . and others don't.* New York: HarperCollins.

Costa, A. L., & Kallick, B. (2000). *Exploring and discovering habits of mind.* Alexandria, VA: ASCD.

Costa, A. L., & Kallick, B. (Eds.). (2000). *Habits of mind: A developmental series.* Alexandria, VA: ASCD.

Dahl, K. A. (2007). *What Is Anthropology?* Retrieved May 16, 2008 from http://www2.eou.edu/%7Ekdahl/what.html

Danielson, C. (1996). *Enhancing professional practice: A framework for teaching.* Alexandria, VA: ASCD.

DuFour, R., & Baker, R. E. (1998). *Professional learning communities at work: Best practices for enhancing student achievement.* National Education Service.

DuFour, R., Eaker, R., & DuFour, R. (2005). *On common ground.* Bloomington, IN: Solution Tree.

Fullan, M. G. (1994). Coordinating top-down and bottom-up strategies for education reform. In R. Anson (Ed.), *Systemic reform: Perspective on personalizing education.* Washington, DC: U.S. Department of Education, Office of Educational Research & Improvement.

Hutchens, D. (2000). *Outlearning the wolves: Surviving and thriving in a learning organization* (2nd ed.). Waltham, MA: Pegasus Communications, Inc.

Jacobs, H. H. (1997). *Mapping the big picture: Integrating curriculum & assessment K–12.* Alexandria, VA: ASCD.

Jacobs, H. H. (2001, Fall). An Interview with Dr. Heidi Hayes Jacobs. *Independent School Magazine,* pp. 18–22.

Jacobs, H. H. (2006). *Getting results with curriculum mapping [Video series].* Alexandria, VA: ASCD.

Kipling, R. (1940). The law of the jungle. In *Rudyard Kipling's verse: definitive edition* (pp. 559–561). Garden City, NY: Doubleday and Company.

Marzano, R., & Kendall, J. (1998). *Awash in a sea of standards.* Denver, CO: McREL.

McDonald, J., Mohr, N., Dichter, A., & McDonald, E. (2003). *The Power of Protocols.* NY: New York Teachers College Press. (This reference provides considerable insight into the development of protocols—the ones used here are variations that have been developed by the authors of this book.)

Newmann, F., & Wehlage, G. (1995). *Successful school restructuring: A report to the public and educators*. Madison, WI: University of Wisconsin Education Center.

Payne, R. (2003, July). How do you develop and measure intellectual capital in school systems (buildings and districts)? (No Child Left Behind (NCLB) Series, Part III). *Instructional Leader, XVI*(4). Retrieved May 16, 2008, from http://www.tepsa.org/Publications/PDF/RubyPayneIII.pdf

Schmoker, M. J. (1996). *Results: The key to continuous school improvement*. Alexandria, VA: ASCD.

Senge, P. (1990). *The Fifth Discipline*. New York: Doubleday.

Silns, H., & Mulford, B. (2002). Leadership and school results. In K. A. Leithwood & P. Hallinger (Eds.), *Second International Handbook of Educational Leadership and Administration*. Dordrecht, The Netherlands: Kluwer Academic Publishers.

Spillane, J. P., Halverson, R., & Diamond, J. B. (2001). Investigating school leadership practice: A distributed perspective. *Educational Researcher, 30*(3).

Stacey, R. (1992). *Managing the Unknowable*. San Francisco: Jossey-Bass.

Stiggins, R. J. (2001). *Student-involved classroom assessment*. Upper Saddle River, NJ: Merrill Prentice Hall.

Udelhofen, S. (2005). *Keys to curriculum mapping: Strategies and tools to make it work*. Thousand Oaks, CA: Corwin Press.

Wiggins, G., & McTighe, J. (1998). *Understanding by design*. Alexandria VA: ASCD.

Index

NOTE: Entries followed by "f" indicate figures; "t" indicate tables.

CORWIN PRESS

The Corwin Press logo—a raven striding across an open book—represents the union of courage and learning. Corwin Press is committed to improving education for all learners by publishing books and other professional development resources for those serving the field of PreK–12 education. By providing practical, hands-on materials, Corwin Press continues to carry out the promise of its motto: **"Helping Educators Do Their Work Better."**